STUDIES IN THE
MAKING OF CITIZENS

MAKING FASCISTS

THE UNIVERSITY OF CHICAGO PRESS, CHICAGO

THE BAKER & TAYLOR CO., NEW YORK; THE MACMILLAN COMPANY OF
CANADA, LIMITED, TORONTO; THE CAMBRIDGE UNIVERSITY PRESS,
LONDON; THE MARUZEN-KABUSHIKI-KAISHA, TOKYO, OSAKA, KYOTO,
FUKUOKA, SENDAI; THE COMMERCIAL PRESS, LIMITED, SHANGHAI

MAKING FASCISTS

By HERBERT W. SCHNEIDER

and

SHEPARD B. CLOUGH

THE UNIVERSITY OF CHICAGO PRESS
CHICAGO · ILLINOIS

8162

EDITOR'S PREFACE

This study of civic education is one of a series of similar analyses of a variety of states. Broadly speaking, the common purpose of these inquiries has been that of examining objectively the systems of civic education in a group of states, of determining the broad trends of civic training in these modern nations, and of indicating possibilities in the further development and control of civic education. In two of these cases, Italy and Russia, striking experiments are now being made in the organization of new types of civic loyalty. Germany, England, the United States, and France present instances of powerful modern states and the development of types of civic cohesion. Switzerland and Austria-Hungary are employed as examples of the difficulty experienced in reconciling a central political allegiance with divergent and conflicting racial and religious elements.

The series includes the following volumes:

Soviet Russia, by Professor Samuel N. Harper, Professor of Russian Language and Institutions in the University of Chicago.

Great Britain, by Professor John M. Gaus, Professor of Political Science, University of Wisconsin.

Austria-Hungary, by Professor Oscar Jaszi, formerly of Budapest University, now Professor of Political Science in Oberlin College.

The United States, by Professor Carl Brinkmann, Professor of Political Economy in the University of Heidelberg.

Italy, by Professor Herbert W. Schneider, Professor of Religion in Columbia University, and Shepard B. Clough, Instructor in History in Columbia University.

Germany, by Mr. Paul Kosok, New York City.

vii

Switzerland, by Professor Robert C. Brooks, Professor of Political Science in Swarthmore College, Swarthmore, Pennsylvania.

France, by Professor Carleton J. H. Hayes, Professor of History in Columbia University. (This is a part of the Columbia University series of "Studies in Post-War France" and is included here because of its intimate relation to the other volumes in the series.)

Civic Attitudes in American Textbooks, by Dr. Bessie L. Pierce, Professor of History in the State University of Iowa.

The Duk-Duks, by Dr. Elizabeth Weber, Professor of Political Science, Hunter College, New York City.

Comparative Civic Education, by Professor Charles E. Merriam, Professor of Political Science in the University of Chicago.

Wide latitude has been given and taken by the individual collaborators in this study, with the understanding, however, (1) that as a minimum there would be included in each volume an examination of the social bases of political cohesion and (2) that the various mechanisms of civic education would be adequately discussed. There is inevitably a wide variation in point of view, method of approach, and in execution of the project. Investigators differ as widely in aptitude, experience, and environment.

Of the various investigations the questions may be asked: What part do the social groupings play in the spirit of the state? What is the attitude of the economic groups which for this purpose may be considered under certain large heads, as the attitude of the business element, of the agricultural group, or of labor? What is the relation of the racial groups toward the political group whose solidarity is in question? Do they tend to integrate or disintegrate the state? What is the position of the religious factors in the given society, the Catholic, the Protestant, the Jewish? How are they related to loyalty toward the political unit? What is the place of the regional groupings in the political unit? Do they develop special tendencies alone or in company with other types of groupings already mentioned? What is the relation of these competing loyalties to each other?

It cannot be assumed that any of these groups has a special attraction or aversion toward government in general; and the analysis is not conducted with any view of establishing a uniformity of interest or attachment in any type of group, but rather of indicating the social composition of the existing political units and authorities. It may well be questioned whether there is any abstract loyalty, political or otherwise. These political loyalties are determined by concrete interests, modified by survivals that no longer fit the case and by aspirations not yet realized. The cohesion is a resultant of conflicting forces, or a balance of existing counterweights, a factor of the situation. All these factors may change and the balance may be the same, or one may change slightly and the whole balance may be overthrown. It is the integration of interests that counts, not the special form or character of any one of them.

Among the mechanisms of civic education which it is hoped to analyze are those of the schools, the rôle of governmental services and officials, the place of the political parties, and the function of special patriotic organizations; or, from another point of view, the use of traditions in building up civic cohesion, the place of political symbolism, the relation of language, literature, and the press to civic education, the position occupied by locality in the construction of a political loyalty; and, finally, it is hoped that an effective analysis may be made of competing group loyalties rivaling the state either within or without.

In these groups there is much overlapping. It would be possible to apply any one or all of the last-named categories to any or all of the first. Thus the formal school system made and does utilize language and literature, or symbolism, or love of locality, or make use of important traditions. Symbolism and traditions may and do overlap—in fact, *must* if they are to serve their purpose; while love of locality and language may be and are interwoven most intimately.

Intricate and difficult of comprehension as some of these patterns are, they lie at the basis of power; and control systems, however crude, must constantly be employed and invented to deal with these situations. The device may be as simple as an ancient symbol or as complicated as a formal system of school training, but in one form or other these cohesive devices are constantly maintained.

In the various states examined, these devices will be traced and compared. The result will by no means attain the dignity of exact measurement but will supply a rough tracing of outlines of types and patterns in different cities. It is hoped, however, that these outlines will be sufficiently clear to set forth some of the main situations arising in the process of political control and to raise important questions regarding the further development of civic education.

It may be suggested that the process by which political cohesion is produced must always be considered with reference to other loyalties toward other groups in the same society. Many of the devices here described are common to a number of competing groups and can be more clearly seen in their relation to each other, working in co-operation or competition, as the situation may be. The attitude of the ecclesiastical group or the economic group, or the racial or cultural group, or any of them,

profoundly influences the nature and effect of the state's
attempt to solidify political loyalty; and the picture is
complete only when all the concurrent or relevant factors
are envisaged.

These devices are not always consciously employed
although they are spoken of here as if they were. It often
happens that these instrumentalities are used without the
conscious plan of anyone in authority. In this sense it
might be better to say that these techniques are found
rather than willed. At any rate, they exist and are operating.

These eight or nine techniques are only rough sched-
ules or classifications of broad types of cohesive influences. They are not presented as accurate analyses of the
psychology of learning or teaching the cohesive process
of political adherence. They presuppose an analysis of
objectives which has not been made, and they presuppose
an orderly study of the means of applying objectives;
and this also had not been worked out in any of the states
under consideration.

The volume on *Making Fascists* by H. W. Schneider
and S. B. Clough is based upon an intimate study of the
background and the workings of the present-day Italian
system. The results of Mr. Schneider's previous re-
searches in Italy during 1927–28 as a Fellow of the Social Science Research Council have already been published in his notable work on *Making the Fascist State*.
Mr. Clough has been a student of Belgium nationalism
under the direction of Professor Hayes, and spent a number of months in 1928 assembling data on the Italian
system of civic training. Approaching the subject from
somewhat different points of view, Schneider as a student
of philosophy (later of religion) and Clough as a histo-

rian, they have pooled their materials and endeavored to obtain a rounded and objective idea of a situation which is often viewed through the distorting lenses of emotion, prejudice, and propaganda. In addition to this, Mr. Schneider and Mr. Clough were able to use the valuable background study of Professor Robert Michels on the history of Italian patriotism. This work which contains important material of a historical nature is expected to appear in a later number of this series.

CHARLES E. MERRIAM

AUTHORS' PREFACE

In undertaking this book the authors were confronted with the task of corralling material which had never before been brought together and which concerned entirely new phenomena in Italian life. From the very first it was apparent that the success of the volume depended largely upon the co-operation of those men who were intimately acquainted with the details of making Fascists, men who were actually taking part in the Fascist experiment. Without exception every request for aid was graciously accorded. Officials of the Fascist party, the presidents of the various confederations, the heads of many Fascist organizations, Fascist journalists, technical advisers to the Régime, members of the bureaucracy, and statesmen gave liberally of their time and knowledge to make this book informative. It is no exaggeration to state that direct contact either by personal interview or by correspondence was made with some leader in every phase of Fascist enterprise. In order that the picture might be a balanced one, the authors also interviewed opponents of the Régime both in Italy and abroad, and thus secured information concerning certain phases of contemporary Italy, as, for instance, concerning South Tyrol and Venetia-Julia, which could not have been acquired in any other way. Personal acknowledgment for the aid obtained would be quite impossible in this place, but the authors wish to take this opportunity to thank all those who assisted them in collecting material.

Finally, the authors wish also to express their appreciation of the assistance given them by Rosina Clough in gathering the material for the book, and by Carol Schneider in the preparation of the manuscript.

SHEPARD B. CLOUGH
HERBERT W. SCHNEIDER

TABLE OF CONTENTS

PART I. GROUP ATTITUDES

I. FASCISM AND ECONOMIC GROUPS 3

II. REGIONAL AND RACIAL DIFFERENCES 24

III. INTERNATIONAL RELATIONS 48

IV. FASCISM AND CATHOLICISM 63

PART II. TECHNIQUES OF CIVIC TRAINING

V. FASCIST EDUCATION 83

VI. MILITARY TRAINING 110

VII. THE BUREAUCRACY 129

VIII. THE FASCIST PARTY 140

IX. THE FASCIST PRESS 159

X. VARIOUS PATRIOTIC ORGANIZATIONS 178

XI. THE USE OF SYMBOLISM AND TRADITION 189

XII. GENERAL SURVEY 199

BIBLIOGRAPHICAL NOTE 205

INDEX 209

PART I
GROUP ATTITUDES

CHAPTER I

FASCISM AND ECONOMIC GROUPS

1. *Economic groups in early Fascism.*—In that it is predominantly agricultural, Fascism more accurately reflects the economic life of Italy than most parties of the past have done. Both in the origins of the movement and in the present policies of the Régime, the agricultural interests of the country have been the strongest force, as they are also the most important factor in Italian national economy. The following figures indicate the relative strength of various economic groups in early Fascism. At the Rome congress of the party, November, 1921, Secretary Pasella reported the following distribution of the party membership:[1]

OCCUPATION	PERCENTAGE OF PARTY MEMBERSHIP
Business men	9
Industrialists	3
Professional men	6
Public employees	5
Private office employees	10
Teachers	1
Students	13
Sailors and marine workers	1
Industrial laborers	16
Agricultural laborers	24
Landowners and tenant farmers	12

At the first national congress of Fascist syndicates, held in June, 1922, the syndicates represented totaled a membership of 458,000, of which 277,000 were from agriculture and only 72,000 from industry.

[1] See P. N. F., *Le Origini e lo sviluppo del Fascismo* (Rome, 1928), pp. 151–52.

3

2. *Fascist labor syndicalism and the corporate state.*
—The attempt of Rossoni, Rocco, and others to establish
an "integralist" syndicalism, based on the doctrine of
class co-operation and on the grouping of the nation not
according to classes but according to economic interests,
led to the organization of "corporations" or "mixed" syndicates. Though this policy met with some initial success
in agriculture, it failed completely in industry. The Confederation of Industry flatly refused to be controlled by
any syndical labor monopoly whatsoever, Fascist or non-
Fascist. The employers had even dared to hope that Fascism spelled the end of all organized labor in Italy. The
compromise (known as the Pact of the Vidoni Palace)
which was finally established (1925) between the Rossoni Confederation of Fascist Syndicates and the Confederation of Industry definitely separated employers
and employees, allowed the right of each to organize, and
recognized the rival confederations as the legal representatives of their respective members.

This set the pattern for subsequent Fascist labor legislation. The basic labor laws are the Law of April 3,
1926, entitled *La Disciplina Giuridica dei Rapporti Col-
lettiva del Lavoro;* the *Regolamento* of June 30, 1926,
which completes the economic organization of the country begun by the former law; the several decrees establishing the Ministry of Corporations; and finally the Parliamentary Reform of February, 1928. Perhaps even
more important than these laws is the general declaration
of labor policy and principles, issued April 21, 1927, and
known as the Labor Charter.[2] We can give here only the
most general provisions of this legislation. They are:

[2] The text of the Labor Charter is given in Herbert W. Schneider, *Making the Fascist State,* p. 332. The most convenient method of getting the labor
legislation, collective contracts, and judicial decisions of the labor tribunals is
to consult the publications of the Ministry of Corporations, especially: (a)

(1) The Fascist syndicates and their confederations are the legal organizations of their various groups, and the only organizations permitted. All persons in these groups are taxed for their support, though membership is not compulsory.

These syndicates are confederated into thirteen national organizations:

a) Employers' organizations: (1) National Fascist Confederation of Industry; (2) National Fascist Confederation of Agriculturalists; (3) National Fascist Confederation of Merchants; (4) National Fascist Confederation of Maritime and Aerial Transportation; (5) National Fascist Confederation of Land Transportation and Inland Navigation; (6) National Fascist Confederation of Bankers.

b) Labor: The National Confederation of Fascist Syndicates, composed of: (7) National Federation of Fascist Syndicates in Industry; (8) National Federation of Fascist Syndicates in Agriculture; (9) National Federation of Fascist Syndicates in Commerce; (10) National Federation of Fascist Syndicates in Maritime and Aerial Transportation; (11) National Federation of Fascist Syndicates in Land Transportation and Inland Navigation; (12) National Federation of Fascist Syndicates in Banks; (13) National Federation of Fascist Syndicates of Intellectuals. The Federations are at present (March, 1929) undergoing reorganization for

---

Disciplina giuridica dei rapporti collettivi del lavoro e ordinamento corporativo dello Stato (Rome: Libreria dello Stato, 1927), No. 619. (*b*) *Il Diritto del Lavoro,* which appears periodically; (*c*) *Atti Ufficiali delle confederazioni nazionali.* Each of the national confederations publishes a series of proceedings, constitutions, collective contracts, etc. For the labor syndicates consult Rossoni's daily, *Il Lavoro d'Italia,* and his monthly, *La Stirpe.* A useful manual is Alberto Pennachio's *The Corporate State* (New York: Italian Historical Society). His *Manuale* in Italian is more comprehensive and up to date.

the purpose of eliminating survivals of pre-Fascist syndicalism and bringing the whole organization under the general pattern of the "corporate state."

(2) The Ministry of Corporations serves as a political unifying agency: It is supposed to co-ordinate and "discipline" the rival confederations of employers and employees and thus to transform syndicalism into the "corporate state." The chief agencies through which the Ministry of Corporations operate are: (a) The Central Bureaus of the Ministry, consisting of experts as well as politicians; (b) The Provincial Economic Councils, composed of experts and responsible to the prefects and local officials of the Ministry of National Economy; (c) The National Council of Corporations. This originated in Intersyndicate Committees, which were emergency measures, instituted to make immediate and drastic action possible in the regulation of prices, wages, rents, and so forth. They are composed partly of representatives of the confederations, partly of party officials. They are appointed by the minister of corporations.

(3) Labor tribunals: These are special courts consisting of experts appointed by the Provincial Economic Councils. Their decisions in labor disputes are obligatory and final.

(4) Collective contracts: These are negotiated by the confederations and regulate labor conditions in detail, not only for syndicate members but for all persons engaged in the occupation covered by the contract. These contracts serve as a legal basis for the operation of the labor tribunals.

(5) Strikes, lockouts, and all forms of class warfare are prohibited.

(6) The Corporate Parliament: According to the new Italian electoral law, the lower House of Parliament

is composed of representatives chosen in the following
manner: The various confederations nominate eight hundred representatives. The Ministry of Corporations and
the Grand Council of the party select four hundred names
from this list of candidates and submit them for approval
or rejection *en bloc* to the syndicate members. In case the
government list should be rejected a machinery is provided whereby the confederations can elect another list of
their own.

It will be noticed from this summary statement of the
framework of the corporate state that the basic pattern is
the separate organization of labor and capital with the
various organs of the government holding the balance,
favoring now one and now the other side, as may be opportune. This process is called, in Fascist phraseology,
"disciplining the syndical organizations in the interests
of the Nation as a whole."

There are several groups which do not fit very neatly
into this scheme: (1) The professional classes, intellectuals, and journalists. It had originally been planned to
make a "third order" out of them. This would have tend-
ed to throw the balance of power into their hands. Both
the labor forces under Rossoni and the Fascist politicians
naturally objected to this. Rossoni finally succeeded in
getting the national confederations of these groups under
his wing. (2) The artisans, small shopkeepers, and farmers. It was at first proposed to split these rather arbitrarily and parcel them out between the capital and labor
syndicates, but neither side wanted them. They were
finally organized as a Communità Autonoma and attached to the Confederation of Industry. (3) The co-operatives. One of the most ironical facts about Fascist economic policy is that the very groups which most directly
embody the principles of Fascist theory have proved the

most difficult to embody in the Fascist state. A group of
Fascists under Gaetano Postiglione succeeded in wrest-
ing the control of the syndicates of co-operatives from the
Socialists and Popularists. Naturally Rossoni wanted to
get the whole co-operative movement under his control,
and the employers' confederations, on the other hand,
would have shed no tears had the whole movement been
destroyed. Nevertheless, the co-operative leaders held
out against both sides and finally (1927) succeeded in establishing by royal decree the Ente Nazionale delle Co-
operazione, an independent body recognized by the state
and protected by the Ministry of Corporations. At the
same time, however, the decree stipulated that the various
federations of co-operatives should be "affiliated" with
whatever syndical confederations most nearly resembled
them. This resulted in a distribution of the federations of
co-operatives among the Confederation of Labor Syndicates, the Confederation of Industry, and the Confederations of Agriculture and Commerce. Thus the co-operatives, though officially independent, are theoretically
embodied in the machinery of the corporate state, and
are hence subject to pressure from all sides. At present
they are strong enough to resist and they enjoy the active
support of the government. Some idea of the relative
strength of the various kinds of co-operatives can be
gained from the following figures. The 4,000 co-operatives, with 400,000 members, are divided thus:

Consumers' co-operatives	1,808
Co-operatives of production and labor .	1,132
Agricultural co-operatives . . .	307
Rural credit co-operatives . . .	350
Building co-operatives	178

In addition there are various co-operative associations for
the marketing of grain, wine, and milk.

In the general effort to better the conditions of the working-classes Fascism has undertaken a wholesale program of social insurance. Previous to the Fascist Revolution, Italy had obligatory accident insurance laws,[3] but they did not function very well. Fascism has endeavored to enforce these laws and has passed new ones making old-age and unemployment insurance obligatory.[4] An organization under the direction of the president of the Confederation of Fascist Syndicates has been created (Il Patronato per l'Assistenza Sociale) for giving legal advice to workers and for enforcing social legislation. Under the pressure of the new order the benefits of social insurance have been greatly increased.[5]

3. *Agriculture.*—The advent of Fascism found agriculture completely disorganized. The peasants belonged to the revolutionary syndicates and labor leagues, which in many regions (notably in Romagna) exercised an effective labor monopoly. The large landowners, traditionally unorganized, were forced after the war to defend themselves and accordingly formed the General Confederation of Agriculture, which by 1922 threatened to become an independent political party. The lower middle class in agriculture, however, whose interests were divided, organized nationalistic syndicates and these affiliated themselves with the Fascist movement. After the March on Rome and the rapid advance of Fascist syndicalism, the General Confederation of Agriculture found its political party aims frustrated and consequently large numbers drifted into the Fascist "mixed," middle-class syndicates. Fearing a new labor monopoly under Rossoni, the large landowners resisted him as best they could and final-

[3] Laws of August 23, 1917, and January 31, 1904.

[4] Decrees of December 30, 1923.

[5] See *Annuario Statistico Italiano* (1928), pp. 288 ff.

ly forced a compromise which has since become the pattern for all Fascist economic organization: the Confederation of Fascist Syndicates was given the official right to defend and organize agricultural labor and the Confederation of Agriculture to defend and organize agricultural employers. These two organizations carry on peaceful collective bargaining, and the courts, the party, and the government constitute a third agent which intervenes decisively in case of conflict. The National Federation of Syndicates of Agricultural Laborers has a membership of about 1,000,000, and the Confederation of Agricultural Employers has about 600,000. All persons engaged in agriculture, however, are taxed for the support of one or the other of these confederations. About a million employers and several times that many employees are thus taxed.

The Confederation of Employees is naturally preoccupied with conditions of labor; it negotiates collective contracts fixing wages, hours, insurance, health regulations, and everything else pertaining to the interests of labor. The Confederation of Employers, on the other hand, is chiefly concerned with the technical organization and progress of agriculture. The elaborate technical bodies, and their highly centralized system of control by experts, are the most distinctive features of the Fascist agricultural policy. In 1923 the Ministry of Agriculture was abolished and fused with other ministries to form the single Ministry of National Economy. This ministry now works directly through the confederations and has succeeded in co-ordinating the all too numerous and hitherto independent agricultural associations into a single system, fixing the responsibilities of each and giving them more power. All the national organizations have their provincial branches.

The departments, into which the technical supervision of agriculture is divided, follow, with mention of some of the important policies and achievements of Fascist administration in each field.

(1) Rural credit: Considerable credit has been extended to farmers, especially in the South where capital is scarce, for the purposes of encouraging wheat-raising and buying farm machinery. The largest credits, however, have gone to

(2) Works of irrigation, drainage, and rural constructions: The South is most in need of such development, and northern capital has been heavily invested in huge agricultural developments, sponsored by the government but conducted by private firms. Large areas are being brought into cultivation. Especially significant are the drainage of large marshes on the western coast and the reclamation of the Roman plains. The productivity of many regions has been enhanced by subsoil plowing with steam plows.

(3) Taxation, customs, tariffs, and philanthropy: A protective tariff on foodstuffs has been revived; municipal customs duties have been extended, and favorable reductions in foreign tariffs have been obtained by the numerous commercial treaties negotiated by the Fascist government.

(4) Agricultural machinery: Many efforts have been made to introduce machinery wherever possible: credit has been offered for the purchase of machinery; public demonstrations, lectures, and motion pictures advertise its uses; industry has been encouraged to increase Italian manufacture of farm machinery, and special schools have been established for mechanical engineering.

(5) Scientific bureaus: There are both national and provincial boards of experts carrying on experiments

and conducting public education in matters of animal husbandry, seed selection, phytopathology, and the like. Proper fertilization has been made compulsory.

(6) Marketing and commercial studies: Improved methods of marketing, exporting, storing, and so forth, are being developed.

(7) Judicial commissions to study legal aspects of land tenure and to look after the legal interests of agriculture: Severe legislation against fraud and adulteration has been passed.

(8) Each of the major agricultural industries has a centralized administration made up for the most part of technical experts and economists: These national organizations are not trusts or monopolies, for private concerns are allowed to compete, but they are tending in that direction; their powers are being continually enlarged and pressure is continually brought to bear on them to increase the national production and income, regardless of special interests. The most important industries thus organized are: silk, wine, milk, fruit, canned goods, olives, sugar cane, sugar beet, tobacco, poultry, bee culture, and water buffalo.

(9) Co-operatives: See above, pages 7–8.

(10) Education: The budget for traveling lectures, demonstrations, and agricultural motion pictures has been increased enormously. New agricultural secondary schools have been established; there is a special school for agricultural mechanics at Rome, and professional studies and degrees for young peasants have been greatly extended. Agricultural education is encouraged by making some sort of professional degree a prerequisite for holding office in any of the provincial or national organizations. The emphasis placed on the political leadership of

technical experts has also stimulated an interest in professional agricultural training.

(11) The press and propaganda: The Confederation of Agriculturalists publishes a weekly paper (which will soon be a daily) called *L'Agricoltura d'Italia* and two monthlies, *L'Italia Agricola* and *Cerere*. These are popular journals. The Sunday paper, *Giornale di Agricoltura di Domenica*, is more technical. Regional and national expositions and fairs are used frequently to stimulate interest.

Most significant at present and most typical of Fascist propaganda is the *Battaglia del Grano* (the battle of wheat), which is one of a series of economic "battles" being waged by the government. Its aim is to increase the per acre yield until Italy raises enough wheat to feed its population. An intensive press campaign is carried on; posters, speeches, and pictures are so constructed as to stimulate rivalry and military enthusiasm in the fields of intensive agriculture. Prizes are offered to the extent of 3,500,000 lire.

Mussolini has taken an active personal interest in the campaign. He has been preaching at length on the theme of "back to the soil" and has announced that the Fascist government places its chief reliance on building up Italy's wealth by building up her agriculture. He has declared that for both moral and economic reasons, Italy should not try to become an industrial power, but that she should lead the world in the science and art of agriculture. To this end he preaches "ruralism," a passionate love for the soil and for rural occupations, and not mere "agriculturism," or mere interest in making a living off the soil. Every means, therefore, is being applied to cultivate literally a love for the country, the land, and the soil, as the very essence of love for the *patria*.

4. *Industry, finance, and commerce.*—The various groups concerned in the industrial, financial, and commercial life of Italy cannot be discussed separately, since their interests and attitudes are interdependent. Nor can any general statement be made regarding their relations to Fascism, for these have changed decidedly in the course of the major fluctuations in Italian economic life during the last few years.

As we have said before, when Fascism first appeared on the scene the lower middle classes were the most active and patriotic supporters of the cause. The unexpected violence of the labor crisis of 1919–20 so frightened shopkeepers, small factory-owners, and businessmen whose financial position was none too secure that they joined the movement in haste and contributed liberally, even frantically, to the *fasci*. But when the labor crisis was over these classes in general settled back into their old political habits, relieved that the storm had blown over.

The big industrialists, on the other hand, though they were slow to welcome Fascism, were its mainstay (financially) during the critical years of 1921 to 1924. They were especially pleased with the reforms of the minister of finance, De Stefani. Being an orthodox economist, he conducted a policy (1) of lowering the state budget by freeing it of many of its functions; (2) of simplifying the taxes and making them more direct and easier to collect; (3) of encouraging the accumulation of capital. Hence he began turning over telephones, telegraphs, etc., to private concerns; he tried to turn over even the railroads, but he met too much Fascist opposition. He abolished inheritance taxes and lowered most of the taxes on wealth and capital. He opposed syndicalism and all government interference in business. Naturally such a program was most welcome to the industrial and commercial classes.

But hardly had they begun to rejoice in this government after their own heart than they were confronted by Fascist syndicalism, by grasping and autocratic party officials, and by the tendency toward economic as well as political dictatorship. They became somewhat suspicious of the new régime and their suspicions were abundantly confirmed in 1925 when De Stefani was forced to resign and his liberalistic policy was, at least in part, repudiated. Thereupon those industrialists who had not already turned toward the Liberals entrenched in the Aventine opposition became critical, to say the least. The only factor which relieved the situation in the eyes of some industrial and commercial groups was the inflation of the currency, which gave business a specious prosperity.

Meanwhile the banks were decidedly cool toward Fascism; so long as De Stefani kept hands off, they made what profits they could out of the inflation and the concurrent speculation. But when De Stefani finally became exasperated with the undue amount of speculation and tried to intervene arbitrarily in the sacred money market, such a loud protest went up and such "financial defeatism" seized the bankers that De Stefani resigned. In his place came a leading member of the Banca Commerciale, Count Volpi. The Volpi régime enjoyed the support of financial circles. His success in reaching a war-debt settlement and his attempts to halt inflation were decidedly in their interest. This policy reached its culmination in the summer of 1926, when he and Mussolini launched a vigorous deflation program.

But this sudden deflation was a hard blow to business and led to renewed hostility among the industrialists and the merchants. Instead of yielding, however, the government enforced its deflation policy to the limit. Direct political control was exercised over rents, prices, wages, and

employment—in short, the government took a direct hand
in the regulation of the economic life of the nation. In
this process now one group, now another, was hit or favored. The whole story is complicated and it is impossible to make generalizations, for the economic situation
changed from day to day and with it the attitudes of the
economic groups changed also. The economics and practical achievements of the Fascist policy are beyond the
scope of this work. Suffice it to say that the crisis came
during the winter of 1927–28 (unemployment, bankrupt-
cies, etc.), but with the spring the figures showed a general upward trend and now the government is quite certain that "the battle is won" and Fascism's prestige
among business circles has risen considerably.

What concerns us here, however, about these events
are the techniques which Fascism has employed in winning the support and loyalty of the various industrial,
financial, and commercial groups. The general Fascist
method of controlling any and all economic groups is
known as the "corporate state." Though this grew directly out of the practical situation we have just described,
we shall postpone a discussion of it until after we have
discussed Fascist labor policy and we shall confine ourselves here to those more specific techniques which directly concern the groups now under discussion.

The organizations which carry on most of the propaganda among these groups are the six National Fascist
Confederations of Employers, especially the Confederation of Industry, the Confederation of Commerce, and
the Confederation of Bankers. Of these three the Confederation of Industry is the oldest and by far the most
influential. These organizations are parallel to the Confederation of Agriculture which we have already discussed, and their activities are of a similar nature. They

control the provincial federations and local syndicates of employers and merchants, and they co-ordinate a large number of national federations, many of which antedate Fascism. The Confederation of Industry, for example, embraces national federations of the following: artisans, industrial managers, machines and metallurgy, lumber, eight federations of agricultural industries, two of mines, five of building materials and construction, ten of textile industries, three of chemical industries, four of paper and printing industries, and nine of various public utilities. These federations all send delegates to the National Council of the Confederation and this Council is under the guidance of a few directors who are constantly and directly in touch with the government. By means of this highly centralized mechanism, with a few prominent Fascist industrialists at its head, the government can effectively and easily spread its propaganda and control over employers generally.

In addition to their functions as syndicates, these national confederations conduct a number of general departments, offices, or sections. Take as an example the Confederation of Commerce. It is composed of the national federations of the following: merchants, touring and travel, leather and shoes, public services, bakers, motion picture theater operators, station restaurants, salesmen, druggist supplies, and insurance agents. To this bizarre list others are being added continually, for this confederation is one of the youngest. But in addition, the confederation maintains the following general offices: (1) administrative office (with four subdepartments), (2) general secretarial staff (eight subdepartments), (3) special office for legislation and commercial consultation (four subdepartments), (4) special office of economics and colonies (five subdepartments). These "offices" carry

on considerable propaganda, but their chief function is to
formulate the needs and interests of the members of the
confederation and to present them to the government for
consideration. Thus they form powerful, centralized lob-
bies through which most of the legislative suggestions
come.

The patriotic appeals made to the employers and merchants by the Fascist organizations can be summarized in
the following general doctrines:

(1) The hardships ensuing from the deflation policy
are a sacrifice which the state demands of all its members,
in order to enable Italy to achieve economic power and international financial credit.

(2) The less efficient firms must go under in the struggle for existence: Italy cannot afford to nurse them and
the government will show no sympathy. It is admitted
that this will probably tend toward a centralization of
power in a few large firms, tending to become national
trusts. But centralization is not a conscious policy; if it
comes, it comes because of its greater efficiency. This is
true only of the big national industries.

(3) On the other hand, there is a large number of
small industries, artisans, and individual entrepreneurs:
This group has its own federation (subordinated to the
Confederation of Industry) and is to be protected and
encouraged on the ground that a poor country like Italy
must necessarily rely to a large extent on its small industries.

(4) Buy domestic products: One of the major concerns of the government is to reduce imports, but this is
not to be achieved by protective tariffs (a short-sighted
policy, which reacts unfavorably on the foreign markets
for Italian goods), but rather by a persistent propaganda appealing to the national loyalty and the moral sense

of the consumer. The propaganda against using foreign goods is carried on by all sorts of agencies—posters, advertising, newspaper editorials, denunciation of foreign fashions, and so forth.

(5) Italian industry must be encouraged to seek foreign markets: Italy's capacity to manufacture exceeds her domestic demand, but she cannot afford to limit herself to the satisfaction of her own needs; her surplus labor needs employment and it can find employment only in an expansive, "imperialistic" industry. Recently the National Institute for Exportation has been revived and enlarged. It enjoys the energetic support of the government and is expected to carry on propaganda in foreign countries for Italian goods.

5. *The civic functions of Fascist syndicalism.*—It is still too early to tell how the corporate state will work. Probably it will soon become the controlling mechanism of Italian economic life. At present its functions are primarily political rather than economic. At worst it is a smoke screen for the arbitrary tampering of Fascist officials and busybodies in economic affairs; at best it is an ingenious mechanism for infusing nationalism into economics. The importance of this last function can hardly be overestimated. Apart from carrying on general Fascist propaganda along with all other Fascist organizations, these syndicates and corporate offices, committees, and councils promote the following forms of training in the interests and affairs of the nation:

(1) Syndicalism, which formerly served anarchism, is made to serve national patriotism: Rossoni's original motto, *La Patria non si nega, si conquista* (Not to deny but to win our country), emphasizes the idea that a militant syndicalism can conquer the state by becoming the state and that hence the love of one's country need not

take the traditional negative form of military sacrifice,
but can take the positive form of co-operative production.
This harnessing of patriotic motives with labor movements, which goes back in Italy at least as far as the *Risorgimento* and, therefore, has a foothold in Italian tradition, has proved to be an idea peculiarly well adapted to
the present economic situation in Italy.

(2) The emphasis on production as the essential mode
of citizenship is another favorite theme of syndicalist
propaganda: The idea cuts both ways: on the one hand,
it opposes the old destructive labor techniques of strikes,
sabotage, etc.; on the other, it attacks the unproductive
bourgeoisie and those forms of investment and income
which do not contribute to the wealth of the nation. Furthermore, the test of productivity, which underlies the
rights of the citizen, is also applied to the government: a
government ceases to be good when it ceases to enhance
the economic power and resources of the nation. This
"imperialistic" conception of labor, which turns even the
humblest emigrant into a missionary of Italian creative
genius, may sound excessively romantic and sentimental
to an outsider, but to an Italian it seems less strange; for
it must be remembered that in Italy, with its constant
surplus of population, labor is a privilege rather than a
burden.

Fascism has attempted to give ceremonial recognition to labor, by granting the title and medal of Knight
of Labor *(Cavaliere di Lavoro)* to laborers who have
worked long and lustily. Hitherto the title, *Cavaliere,*
was obtained only by factory-owners, landed proprietors,
and the upper bourgeoisie, who had performed some very
singular service, or who held office, or who could afford to
buy the honor from their deputies and senators.

(3) Interclass solidarity is preached in the interests

of international struggle: This militant touch of the doctrine of class co-operation is typical of Fascism. The régime knew very well it could do little in the way of preaching peace and prosperity to the Italian proletariat. Therefore it faced hard times frankly and appealed to the people to make sacrifices for Italy's economic warfare. All the techniques used during the war were revived, from loan posters to war bread, and the whole atmosphere was dominated by the "permanent state of war" idea. The eight-hour day was rescinded temporarily and when the deflation made a wage reduction necessary, the people were called upon to make "sacrifices" of from 10 to 20 per cent, while the cost of living went down only 9 per cent. All this was explained at length as the inevitable consequence of foreign financial pressure and international competition. Italy as a whole, they said, is a proletarian nation, waging a class struggle.

(4) The continual intervention of the state by means of the syndicates in the details of daily life is another source of civic training: Every day the papers print lists of persons fined for selling or buying before or after the legal hours; for leaving meats or fruits uncovered in their shops; for keeping open on a holiday; for selling at prices other than the official prices marked on the goods or posted in the shop, etc.—there are a hundred and one petty ways in which a person is continually reminded of the ever-present state. Prices on staples are regulated systematically. There are fees and taxes wherever one turns. Occasionally a farmer will be forced to hire labor which he does not need, or a factory to keep open at a loss. In short, the evidences of collective regulation are so obvious that one does not need to read economics books to know that the laissez-faire politics has gone by the boards.

(5) The most systematic expression of collective reg-

ulation is the collective contract negotiated by the Confederations of Syndicates and binding both on syndicate members and others: Neither the employer nor the employee is free to conduct his own affairs. On the whole the laborers have supported these contracts more willingly than the capitalists, even when wages have been reduced; for every laborer understands perfectly that his syndicate is his only defense against the dictatorship of the employer. The consequent power and importance of the syndicates has succeeded in stimulating popular interest in them to an amazing degree. The *mentalita sindacale,* which is supposed to be the psychological prerequisite for the new political and economic order, is growing rapidly. The masses have been accustomed to the idea for some time; the bourgeoisie is now beginning to feel its import.

(6) Most important of all, perhaps, is the fact that the syndicate is the only institution left in which there is any democracy: Practically all the constitutions of the Fascist syndicates and their confederations enable the individual member to participate in the decisions of his syndicate and thus in the pursuit of his economic interests. The delegates to the Provincial Federal Councils are elected by balloting in the syndicates and the Provincial Councils in turn elect the members of the National Councils, which in turn elect the directors. This is in striking contrast to the organization of the party and the bureaucracy. Of course, the voting is so indirect and power so centralized that the individual syndicate member has little real power; nevertheless, the member is allowed to feel that his participation in the state as a citizen must come through the syndicate. The new Corporate Parliament further strengthens this idea, for only syndicate members can vote and they vote for economic representatives.

Naturally the syndicates at present are run rather high-handedly and constitute the happy hunting-ground for Fascist office-seekers; but this situation is bound to change soon and then either the Fascist Régime will feel the power of democratic syndicates or else the Fascist party will disregard the syndicate constitutions and will include the whole syndical machinery in the dictatorship. In any event, the civic functions of the syndicates are so conspicuous that political interest and the popular imagination are already centered on the "corporate state" rather than on the Fascist party.

CHAPTER II
REGIONAL AND RACIAL DIFFERENCES

1. *Regional patriotism.*—Italian nationalism can be properly estimated only against a background of provincialism. Even the Catholic church has not been untouched by local tradition. The very names of such universal saints as St. Francis of Assisi, St. Catherine of Siena, and St. Anthony of Padua betray their local origins, and there are many lesser patron saints who are little more than symbols of local loyalties and objects of local cults.

Political patriotism, even more than religious, is dominated by local traditions. The fact that Italy has been unified so recently is an obvious, though minor, cause of this absence of national patriotism. Massimo d'Azelio's famous slogan, "Now that we have made Italy, we must make Italians," is still largely unfulfilled, except in so far as Fascism may be regarded as a fulfilment, for the masses of the people are not accustomed to think of themselves as Italians but as Tuscans, Romans, Neapolitans, or Sicilians, and so on. Especially the peasants of the various provinces have little feeling of a common bond among them. Each city, moreover, wants to be *the* center of Italy. For the average peasant there are many "foreign" parts in Italy, and his primary affections are for his region rather than for the *patria* as a whole. Even the textbooks used in the schools reflect considerable regionalism.[1]

Conscious of this fact, Fascist leaders are making

[1] Cf. chap. v.

every conceivable effort to impress the middle-class and intellectualist idea of Italian nationality on the masses. Mussolini's use of the term *il popolo d'Italia* is an obvious illustration. The persistent reference to the sacrifices of the war as the symbol of the final fusion of Italian blood is another. It is interesting to note how even the mention of *risorgimento* heroes, like Mazzini and Garibaldi, arouses *local* patriotism in very much the same way as the mention of Thomas Jefferson in a Democratic convention in the United States. At one time Fascism was almost shipwrecked (at least intellectually) because each local leader sought to champion his own particular favorite as *the* predecessor of Fascism. Much bitter debate centered about the "historic orientation" of the movement; the real point at issue was usually not the truth about history but the importance of some locality. For this reason there is a concerted effort on the part of the leaders to make Fascism seem something fresh, all-inclusive, and national—or else a resurrection of the ancient unity of Rome. So also national celebrations are made to eclipse local ones; national news is featured in the press, and national needs are preached continually as being of prime concern. The current doctrine of the solidarity of the Italian people is, to be sure, immediately directed against doctrines of class struggle and internationalism, but it is no less directed against the persistent opinion that North and South, industry and agriculture, the "progressive" and the "antique" areas of Italy have divergent interests and aims.

Against such a background the common boast of Fascist orators that "Fascism is Italy" and "the cause of Italy is identical with the cause of Fascism" may, perhaps, sound less like idle phrases and more like a recognition of the importance of conceiving Italy as a nation and not as a "geographic expression" for really distinct regions.

2. *The regional distribution of Fascism.*—Table I summarizes the general facts of the strength of Fascism in the various regions of Italy. The party figures are, of

TABLE I

GEOGRAPHICAL VARIATIONS OF FASCIST PARTY ENROLMENT, 1923–27

Regions (and Chief Cities)	Approx. Pop. (1926)	Pop. per Sq. Kilometer	Party Membership			Percentage of Pop. in Party			Changes in Party Percentage over 1923	
			1923	1924	1927	1923	1924	1927	1924	1927
Northwest:										
Piedmont (Turin)...	3,450,000	117	46,500	39,500	89,500	1.3	1.1	2.5	−0.2	+0.8
Liguria (Genoa).....	1,379,000	253	19,500	16,000	27,000	1.4	1.1	2.0	−0.3	+0.6
Lombardy (Milan)...	5,261,000	221	100,000	79,000	133,000	1.9	1.5	2.6	−0.4	+0.7
Northeast:										
Venetia-Tridentina (Trento).........	666,000	48	4,000	4,000	10,000	.6	.6	1.6	0	+1.0
Venetia (Venice)....	4,402,000	156	46,500	40,000	75,500	1.1	.9	1.7	−0.2	+0.6
Venetia Julia (Trieste)	767,000	127	13,000	8,000	16,000	1.7	1.0	2.1	−0.7	+0.4
Emilia-Romagna (Bologna).........	3,152,000	142	69,000	52,000	84,500	2.2	1.6	2.7	−0.8	+ .5
Center:										
Tuscany (Florence)..	2,853,000	124	82,500	65,000	108,500	2.9	2.4	3.9	−0.5	+1.0
Marches (Ancona)...	1,203,000	124	12,000	9,000	17,000	1.0	.7	1.4	−0.3	+0.4
Umbria (Perugia)....	663,000	79	14,500	7,000	16,000	2.2	1.0	2.4	−1.2	+0.2
Latium (Rome).....	1,740,000	130	36,000	21,000	48,000	2.1	1.2	2.8	−0.9	+0.7
Abruzzi (Aquila)....	1,512,000	91	37,500	22,500	59,000	2.5	1.5	3.9	−1.0	+1.4
South:										
Campania (Naples)..	3,756,000	231	45,000	34,000	85,000	1.2	.9	2.3	−0.3	+0.9
Puglie (Bari)........	2,448,000	128	35,000	24,000	47,000	1.6	1.0	1.9	−0.6	+0.3
Basilicata (Potenza).	495,000	50	11,000	5,500	13,500	2.2	1.1	2.7	−1.1	+0.5
Calabria (Cosenza)..	1,618,000	107	19,000	10,000	40,500	1.2	0.6	2.5	−0.6	+1.3
Sicily (Palermo).....	4,268,000	166	25,000	31,000	49,000	0.6	0.7	1.2	+0.1	+0.6
Sardinia............	916,000	38	8,000	5,500	39,500	0.9	0.6	4.3	−0.3	+3.4
Colonies............					1,650					
Dalmatia............					1,275					
Total...............			630,000 + 150,000 Nationalists	474,500	960,500					

course, not very accurate and all the figures are approximate only. The population figures are calculated for 1926, but the variations between the census of 1921 and the figures here given are not enough to affect the percentages in the last columns.

These figures, in addition to showing the present distribution, indicate the fact that Fascism has changed its local complexion somewhat during the last few years. The general drift of these changes can be summarized as shown in Table II.

The 1923 figures, and to a lesser extent the more recent ones, show that Fascism has its primary stronghold in the central agricultural region of Italy from Emilia-Romagna through Tuscany, Umbria, and the Abruzzi to

TABLE II

SUMMARY OF REGIONAL STRENGTH OF FASCIST PARTY

REGIONS IN ORDER OF POPULATION, FROM MOST POPULOUS TO LEAST (CHIEF CITIES IN PARENTHESES)	REGIONS IN ORDER OF FASCIST PARTY MEMBERSHIP (DEVIATIONS FROM RANK IN POPULATION COLUMN SHOWN IN THE + AND − COLUMNS)					
	1923		1924		1926	
1. Lombardy (Milan)	1	0	1	0	1	0
2. Venetia (Venice)	5	−3	5	−3	6	−4
3. Sicily (Palermo)	10	−7	7	−4	8	−5
4. Campania (Naples)	6	−2	6	−2	4	0
5. Piedmont (Turin)	4	+1	4	+1	3	+2
6. Emilia-Romagna (Bologna)	3	+3	3	+3	5	+1
7. Tuscany (Florence)	2	+5	2	+5	2	+5
8. Puglie (Bari)	9	−1	8	0	10	−2
9. Latium (Rome)	8	+1	10	−1	9	0
10. Calabria (Potenza)	12	−2	12	−2	11	−1
11. Abruzzi (Aquila)	7	+4	9	+2	7	+4
12. Liguria (Genoa)	11	+1	11	+1	13	−1
13. Marches (Ancona)	15	−2	13	0	14	−1
14. Sardinia	17	−3	17	−3	12	+2
15. Venetia-Julia (Trieste)	14	+1	14	+1	15	0
16. Venetia-Tridentina (Trent)	18	−2	18	−2	18	−2
17. Umbria (Perugia)	13	+4	15	+2	16	+1
18. Basilicata (Cosenza)	16	+2	16	+2	17	+1
Mean deviations	2.4		1.9		1.8	

Rome, and a secondary stronghold in the northwestern industrial centers from Turin to Milan. The significance of this geographical distribution for various economic groups is discussed in the previous chapter; it remains for us here to describe certain social groups and non-economic factors which are involved.

3. *Some local variations.*—In the Valley of the Po the social and political situation out of which Fascism

arose was very complicated. In the cities the unified Socialist party had strengthened its grip on local administration and by 1919 was complete master of municipal
government. In the rural districts, the so-called "Red
Labor Leagues" of the Confederazione Generale del Lavoro (C.G.L.) had obtained a similar monopoly. Between these two radical organizations, the one based on
Marxian socialism and the other on Sorelian syndicalism,
there had always been a bitter rivalry for leadership in
the proletarian movement. The situation was further
complicated in 1919, when the Popularist party began
organizing its "white" syndicates. Meanwhile the bourgeoisie was also divided into rival parties: the lower middle class was the stronghold of Republicanism; the large
landholders and capitalists, on the other hand, were Nationalists. The Republicans were revolutionists in the
sense that they opposed the existing monarchical house
and régime; the Nationalists were monarchists and in
general conservatives in everything except foreign policy. What happened during the crisis of 1919 and 1920
was that both Republicans and Nationalists sponsored a
patriotic syndicalism to undermine both the "white" and
the "red" syndicates; and they used Socialist "bosses" or
politicians, who had their own grudges against syndicalism, to organize the *fasci* for doing whatever "dirty work"
was necessary in cleaning up the "reds" and "whites."
These *fasci* were at first under the leadership of the Nationalists and wore blue shirts—supplementing the Gari-
baldine "red shirts." When the Fiume issue arose in the
midst of all this agitation, further complicating the situation, special bands of Blue Shirts and veterans organized the black-shirted *arditi,* who, under the leadership of
d'Annunzio and Ronchi, marched on Fiume. Gradually
the Black Shirts crowded out the Blues, since they were

more symbolical of patriotic and military devotion to Italy and less of internal class warfare and partisan reaction. And gradually the various party groups were fused into two hostile camps: the *blocchi nazionali* against the powerful Socialist and Popularist parties. But even this picture is composite, so to speak, and is much oversimplified. In some cities the fight was between Socialists and Popularists; in others between Nationalists and Socialists; in others between Republicans and Socialists; in others between reformist Socialists and revolutionary Syndicalists, and in still others between landlords and their peasants. In general, however, it is true that Fascism in Romagna was frankly a violent defense of various special interests under the leadership of the Nationalists in the face of the threatened revolution.

In Milan the political climate was considerably different. The Fascists there, under the leadership of Mussolini, were mostly young men from the lower middle classes—students, office employees, war veterans, and young intellectuals—who were radicals and revolutionists but extremely patriotic. They were proletarian radicals on internal issues but ardent nationalists on foreign policy. Mussolini, who had been forced out of Romagna and had taken refuge in Milan, was fairly typical of them —a champion of the war, imperialist, an anti-internationalist, supporter of the Fiume expedition, violent enemy of the liberal government and the bourgeois classes and parties, preacher of revolution and prophet of a rejuvenated *popolo d'Italia* rising in arms against its oppressors at home and abroad. Such proletarian troubadours were flanked by the futurist *fasci,* under the leadership of Marinetti, who attempted to carry the wild unrestraint and revolutionary aims of their art into politics. They were the sworn enemies of everything traditional, convention-

al, and authoritarian; fiercely anticlerical, despising the
prevalent German educational and intellectual traditions
in Italy, and opposed by principle to "law and order."

This Milan Fascism found little proletarian sympathy and still less bourgeois support. It remained a small
band of intellectuals and journalists, who fired the imagi-
nations of students and afforded amusement to others.
Mussolini, however, was quick to sense the direction
which events were taking elsewhere and within a year or
two he had adjusted himself mentally and extended his
leadership over Fascism throughout the nation.

There was a slightly different variety of Fascism in
Florence. Like Milan, Florence was a center for the intellectuals of the movement and Fascism found its chief
support among students, professors, lawyers, journalists, and the sons of landlords and businessmen. But this
Tuscan group was less revolutionary. There were some
Syndicalist and Republican elements in it, but the majority came from the ranks of the Nationalists and Liberals. Behind it was the tradition of the *Voce* movement,
of Italian idealistic philosophy and literature, and, in general, the patriotic tradition of Florence. The d'Annunzian movement found many ardent supporters here and
for a time Florentine Fascism was split into d'Annunzian
and Mussolinian factions. On the whole, patriotic, rather
than strictly economic, issues came to the foreground.
This was especially true of the strong student and veteran elements.

The veterans, in Florence and in other places, too,
were a fairly distinct element. It was from their ranks
that most of the squadrists came. The Florentine squad
was especially notorious. Led by Dumini and a few other
youths of unusual "courage," this squad spread terror
throughout the region and in a short time broke up the

Socialist and Communist organizations. In this connection we might mention the various techniques used by the squadrists in converting Socialists to patriotism. A common method was the breaking up of "red" parades; the ranks were broken, the flags and standards captured, and general disorder created until police or soldiers put an end to it. Occasionally the squadrists would start a parade of their own, thus challenging attack and frequently inviting bloodshed. In general, wherever red flags were hoisted, the squadrists attempted to pull them down and raise the tricolor. Then there were more systematic "punitive expeditions," usually into small villages by night. A few automobile loads of squadrists would drive to the local labor headquarters, usually the chamber of labor, and would start firing more or less at random; if serious fights ensued, they usually burned the building and killed the labor leaders. Less strenuous methods were used on individuals who carried on Communist propaganda. The most typical punishment for these was a severe beating with clubs *(manganelo)*, frequently resulting in permanent injury or even death. Castor oil was administered liberally. Occasionally Communist orators would have their heads shaved and painted with the tricolor. Severe reprisals were always taken for the mistreatment or death of any of their own number. Occasionally squadrists undertook economic warfare by beating up merchants when they refused to lower prices, by "planting the tricolor among the vegetables" in the market, and bringing pressure to bear on the peasants to sell at lower and fixed prices. In fact, intimidation was used for all sorts of purposes. In addition to Florence, the worst centers of such violence were Pisa, Bologna, Modena, Turin, and many smaller towns in the regions around these cities.

There are other minor variations in Fascism into

which it is impossible to enter here. Of the situation in Piedmont (Turin) we have spoken in chapter i. It is interesting to note that Venetia ranks quite low on the Fascist scale. The reason is that this region was the stronghold of the Popularist party, which was the last of the opposition parties to be dislodged. Furthermore, since socialism and communism were relatively weak there, the Nationalist reaction was less violent and formidable than in the neighboring regions. The same is true, curiously enough, of Rome itself. The effect of the "purification" policy and the "dissidence" can be seen readily in the statistics for 1924, given above, and the way it affected particular regions (for example, Umbria) is indicated by the changes in rank of party strength.

4. *The South.*—The chief regional division of Italy is, of course, that between North and South. If figures of 1919 were available they would show even more clearly than the later figures given above that Fascism was in its origins a northern product. Puglie, where organized agricultural labor had made some headway, was about the only southern region seriously involved in the Fascist conflicts. Immediately after the march on Rome the Fascist ranks swelled rapidly and the movement took hold in the South as well. In Sicily Fascism has met with the least success. Many factors have contributed to the comparative indifference of the South. The economic factors, perhaps the most significant, have been discussed in another chapter. Of the other factors, perhaps the chief is the religious. Democratic politics and the secular state never got much foothold in the South, nor did foreign cultures make much of an impression. The social and intellectual life of the people was dominated by the church. After the war, politics made some headway, by means of the Popularist party; but on the whole the South was too

Catholic even for Don Sturzo's party. Politics was conducted almost exclusively by local bosses, who had little to do with the national parties. The upper classes, to be sure, were interested in politics, but they were devoted not so much to the imperialistic sort of nationalism represented by the Fascists and the Nationalist party of the North as to the liberalistic nationalism of the *risorgimento*. Naples had played a leading rôle during the process of national unification and has ever since been a stronghold of liberalism, democracy, and idealism. But the bourgeois and intellectual groups who participated in these movements hardly represented the southern people at large and they played a rather indecisive rôle in the Fascist movement. In fact, the most serious disturbances in the South took place between the Nationalists and the Fascists, who, in the North, were in intimate alliance. A number of Nationalist upper-class veterans, when they returned from the war, organized *fasci,* which were evidently operating in a very reactionary way for the special interests of the big landlords and against the Catholic Popularist party. When the regular Fascists came upon the scene, they found these Nationalist groups already intrenched and unwilling to surrender their leadership. Hence with a double foe, the Nationalists on the one hand, and the Popularists on the other, the Fascist politicians made slow progress.

To make matters all the more difficult, the Fascists tried to win the South by sending down an army of northern politicians, instead of by using what local talent they could rely upon. This brought the traditional enmity between North and South into play. In Sicily the situation was complicated by such local and well-established political forces as the Mafia, which had dominated and terrorized the country around Palermo for generations. Fascism has only recently felt strong enough to attempt a thoroughgoing house-cleaning in Sicily and to wage open warfare against the Mafia. How effective this campaign has been is hard to tell at present. But in theory, at least, the South is now nationalized and local politics is under the complete control of the central government.

A southern association, which has received Fascist approval though it is not a partisan Fascist body is L'Associazione Nazionale per gli Interessi del Mezzogiorno, founded in 1909 in order to raise the social standards of the South. It subsidizes 151 schools and 177 libraries, conducts 586 night schools, furnishes medical advice, and publishes books concerning the problems of southern Italy. Its budget for 1926 was 9,986,055 lire. Patriotic southern pride is stimulated by this association concerned with reforming the South on northern patterns, but at the same time with preventing northern interests from getting control.

5. *South Tyrol.*—Of all the regional problems which confront modern Italy the gravest is that of South Tyrol. For centuries this territory and the province of Trent have been bones of contention between German and Romance peoples. Political boundaries have never coincided with linguistic frontiers, and consequently the growth of modern political nationalism has given rise to irredentist claims. Prior to the World War many Italian-speaking people in the province of Trent were ruled by Austria-Hungary and there was intense Italian irredentist propaganda to "free" this population, but only the wildest Italian nationalists dreamed of annexing South Tyrol, which is primarily German in its culture and language. According to the Austrian census of 1910, the total population of South Tyrol was 257,190, of whom 223,659 spoke German, 22,576 spoke Italian or Ladino (a Ro-

mance dialect), and 10,965 spoke other languages. The Italian census of 1921 stated that there were 193,537 German-speaking Italian citizens, 24,505 foreigners (mostly German and Austrian), and 42,706 Italian- or Ladino-speaking persons (about 16,800 of the latter). Nevertheless Italy entered the war with the promise (the London Pact) that in case of victory the Italian frontier would be established at the Brenner. At the Peace Conference Italy's delegates had great difficulty in convincing President Wilson[2] of the advisability of including South Tyrol in the Italian kingdom, for he was trying to draw boundaries on nationalist lines. Despite his opposition the frontier was finally established at the Brenner, chiefly for strategic reasons. The tables had been turned. The act which redeemed *Italia irredenta* created an *irredenta* for Austria. The news was received with dismay both in South Tyrol and in Austria.

The policy of the Italian government was announced as follows:

The people of other nations who are united with us must know that the idea of oppression and denationalization is foreign to us, and that their languages and cultural institutions will be respected, and that their administrative officials will possess all the privileges of our liberal and democratic legislation.

The king in his address from the throne, December 1, 1919, approved this policy: "The new territory annexed to Italy places new problems before us. Our liberal traditions teach us to solve these problems by respecting, so far as possible, local autonomous institutions and customs."

In the first years of Italian rule in South Tyrol, Italy adhered, for the most part, to the policy outlined in these statements. When the military régime of the first

[2] Ray Stannard Baker, *Woodrow Wilson: Life and Letters,* II, 101.

months ended and a civil authority was established, the
general commissary who was appointed (Professor Credaro, of Rome) was sympathetic with the cultural demands of the people.[3]

Nevertheless the policy of cultural autonomy had its
opponents. Their intellectual leader was Dr. Ettore Tolomei, a former Trent irredentist, who preached the Italianization of South Tyrol and outlined the steps necessary for its realization. There was a severe struggle
between these two policies and, despite the fact that both
Premier Giolitti[4] and Premier Bonomi[5] favored the cultural autonomy policy, there was a gradual drift in the
direction of the Italianization policy.

In 1921 the first general election was held in the new
provinces and the first opportunity given the German
population to declare its attitude toward the Italian state.
For electoral purposes two districts were created—the
one composed almost entirely of German-speaking people (Bolzano, formerly Bozen), the other of Italian- and
Ladino-speaking people (Trent).[6] For the first election
the parties in South Tyrol, with the exception of the Social Democrats, united in a German bloc. They protested
against the annexation and demanded political and cultural autonomy. Of the 46,192 votes·cast in the Bolzano
district, this bloc, known as the Edelweiss, secured 36,-
666, as against the 4,000 of the Social Democrats, thus
electing all its candidates.[7] Further evidence of the gen-

[3] Paul Herre, *Die Südtiroler Frage* (Munich: C. H. Beck, 1927), pp.
123–26.

[4] Paul Herre, *op. cit.*, p. 163.

[5] Speech at the Chamber of Deputies, July 10, 1921.

[6] Decrees of March 10, 1921.

[7] *Statistica delle Elezioni Generali Politiche per la XXVI Legislatura, 15
Maggio, 1921* (Rome: Grafia, 1924).

eral discontent was given in the local elections of 1922, when the German parties won in every town except one.

The astonishing results of these elections and the fear caused by the Anschluss movement[8] gave rise to renewed efforts to subdue the anti-Italian feeling. A decree was issued, September 9, 1921, which made the Italian law of military service applicable in the new province—a change which was particularly distasteful to the people. Moreover, the Corbino School Law, of August 28, 1921, made it obligatory for Italian-speaking families to send their children to Italian schools. The purpose of this act was not alone, as was claimed, to give education in the mothertongue but to prepare the way for the creation of Italian schools for German-speaking children. On January 20, 1921, a decree was issued creating a commission for the Italianization of the names of towns. In the face of such a movement the general commissary, Credaro, lost much of his former prestige and it was suggested that he resign.

While this development was going on the Fascist party was organizing its forces. A *fascio* was established in Trent in 1919 and one in Bolzano in 1921. The first conspicuous act of these organizations was to use bombs to disperse a costume procession in Bolzano on April 24, killing one person and wounding fifty.[9] Mussolini took the moral responsibility for this act[10] and stated that this was only a "holiday warning" of what might happen.[11] A "Parliamentary Group for Vigilance over the Upper Adige" sprang up in the Chamber. It was composed of Mussolini and Nationalists such as Rocco and Federzoni. At every opportunity they preached the Italianization of

[8] Paul Herre, *op. cit.,* p. 188.

[9] Paul Herre, *op. cit.,* p. 187.

[10] Speech in the Chamber, June 21, 1921.

[11] *Popolo d'Italia,* April 25–26, 1921.

South Tyrol, the union of the provinces of Bolzano and Trent, the dismissal of Credaro, the disbanding of German societies, and the realization of bilingualism.[12]

Such was the situation when the Fascists started their coup d'état and, curiously enough, they began by seizing Bolzano on October 1 and 2, 1922. They took the town hall and other government buildings and dismissed the officials. By the end of October they had taken control of Rome and were soon to try their hands at applying their program to the new provinces.

The keynote of the new policy was the Italianization of South Tyrol. Senator Tolomei outlined the necessary measures in a speech delivered at Bolzano, June 15, 1923. He suggested the following reforms:

(1) The union of South Tyrol and Trent in a single province.

(2) The appointment of town mayors by the Italian state.

(3) The revision of the laws concerning the naturalization of foreigners in South Tyrol.

(4) The use of Italian in administrative affairs.

(5) The disbanding of German societies.

(6) The prohibition of the use of the German term, *Süd-Tirol,* and suppression of the German paper, *Der Tiroler.*

(7) The Italianization of the names of people, places, and streets.

(8) The removal of the statue of Walther von der Vogelweide from the principal square in Bolzano.

(9) The strengthening of the Carabinieri in South Tyrol.

(10) The stimulation of Italian immigration to South Tyrol.

[12] Speech by Mussolini in the Chamber, June 21, 1921.

(11) The introduction of the Italian language and culture.

(12) The establishment of Italian kindergartens and the development of Italian elementary and secondary schools.

(13) Strict control of university degrees obtained abroad.

(14) Strict control of the activity of the clergy.

(15) Control of the Chamber of Commerce, of Bolzano.

(16) The use of Italian as the official language in the courts.

(17) The concentration of large bodies of troops in South Tyrol.

This program served as an official guide for the Fascists. One of the first steps of the new government was to unite South Tyrol and Trent in one province with a capital at Trent and to apply all Italian laws concerning provincial and town governments to the new province.[13] It was hoped that the former provision would bring South Tyrol under the Italianizing influence of Trent but the result was not satisfactory and, in 1926,[14] South Tyrol was again transformed into a single province "to hasten the Italianization of the land."[15] This change enabled the Fascists to diminish the local authority of provinces and towns and to concentrate all power in the hands of the national government. The laws which gave the state the right to name the *podestà* (the mayors),[16] and the general increase of the power of the prefects[17] deprived the

[13] Decree of January 21, 1923.

[14] Decree of December 6.

[15] Declaration made by Mussolini, May 26, 1927.

[16] February 4, April 15, and June 25, 1926.

[17] See the Circular to the Prefects, January 5, 1926.

people of local self-government. The result was that the state has been able to do whatever it pleases to realize its plan of Italianization and the people have been unable to defend themselves. In the same manner the syndicalist laws have been applied to draw many of the inhabitants of South Tyrol into the network of the Italian state.[18] The Fascist party has organizations throughout the province but its membership is only a small percentage of the voting population—1,800 as against 8,000 for Trent.[19]

Since the Fascists have held sway in South Tyrol there has been a systematic attack on the German language. All public writings—manifestos, notices, inscriptions, time-tables, etc.—must be in Italian (German is not even permitted on tombstone inscriptions), although in certain districts German translations may accompany the Italian.[20] The official administrative language in South Tyrol is Italian.[21] Whereas some of the former public servants still hold their positions and are able to use German when necessary, many of them have been replaced by Italians who know no German. The complications arising from the inability of post-office clerks, railway guards, customs officials, etc., to make themselves understood are innumerable. Italian is used exclusively in the courts unless one of the parties has absolutely no knowledge of it. Even then the lawyer may not address a question to his client in German but must pose it in Ital-

[18] The excursions to Rome, planned and financed by the syndicates for its members, are examples of the propaganda carried on by these organizations in South Tyrol. In April, 1928, 500 teachers, 115 employers and employees of various callings, and in July of the same year, 500 wounded veterans of the war made patriotic pilgrimages to Rome.

[19] *Foglio d'Ordini,* July 6, Anno V (1927).

[20] Decree of the Prefect of Trent, October 28, 1923, and Decree of the Prefect of Bolzano, November 16, 1927.

[21] Royal Decree of October 13, 1923.

ian through an official interpreter.[22] Moreover, a vigorous attempt is being made to Italianize the names in South Tyrol. The German *Süd-Tirol* is prohibited.[23] A commission directed by Senator Tolomei has been busy changing the names of towns and rivers into Italian forms, with most curious results. An attempt has even been made to Italianize family names, and, although this is not compulsory, one occasionally reads in the official gazette of the Province of Bolzano lists of changes. Fuchs becomes Volpe; Windischgratz, Calonna; Stein, Pietri; Bischof, Bisofi, etc.[24]

Of all the agencies at the disposal of the Fascists for Italianizing South Tyrol, the most important are undoubtedly the schools. The Gentile Reform prescribed that all elementary education be given in Italian and, as a result, German is gradually being excluded from the schools.[25] Italian is used in kindergartens,[26] elementary schools, and in most of the secondary schools, and the teachers are, for the most part, Italians from the south. In order to force students to attend Italian, rather than German or Austrian, universities a law has been made refusing recognition of foreign degrees obtained by inhabitants of the annexed districts, and as a further impediment, serious passport difficulties confront students of South Tyrol who would go abroad.[27] How the schools are used to glorify the Italian nation will be described in another chapter, and no further mention is necessary here. The school problem has created considerable discontent

[22] Decree of October 15, 1925.

[23] Decree of Prefect of Trent, August 8, 1923.

[24] Decree of January 10, 1926.

[25] Gentile Reform, law of October 1, 1923, Art. 31.

[26] Decree of the school authorities of Trent, May 3, 1924.

[27] Royal Decree of September 30, 1923.

and attempts have been made to furnish private tutors and to form secret classes for the instruction of German. Needless to say, such tutors have been persecuted and the classes disbanded whenever discovered, and their influence has not been very great. How effective the schools are in winning the youth is as yet difficult to estimate, but it is certain that some progress is being made.

As part of their program to stamp out opposition and to hinder the use of German, the Fascists have placed a severe curb on the press. The strongest local paper, *Der Tiroler,* has been proscribed. It was reorganized as the *Landsmann* and appeared for a time, but was finally abolished "for stimulating mistrust and hate among the German-speaking population and hindering fraternal relations between the two peoples." At a certain period there was not a single German daily appearing in South Tyrol, all of them having been suspended for political reasons. The main organ of the opposition in Bolzano is at present the *Dolomiten,* which appears three times a week. How severe the censorship is may be gathered from a few copies of this journal. The most it dares to do is to refuse to publish certain of the nationalist articles distributed by the Stefani news agency. The Fascist press in South Tyrol is worthy of note. In 1926 a Fascist daily in German was begun at Bolzano—the *Alpenzeitung*—for Fascist propaganda. An Italian edition of the sheet was started a little later—*La Provincia di Bolzano*—these two papers being the newspaper weapons of the Régime in this province.

It is impossible in the scope of this short study to go into every detail of the means used to Italianize South Tyrol, but the mere mention of some others is necessary. It should be noted, for instance, that military service affords the Italians a chance to teach the youth the Italian language. Tyrolese boys are sent for a year or more into some other Italian district (they almost never serve at home) and by means of their relations with the people and their comrades they get some knowledge of Italian. Another method of Italianization is by means of the church. Realizing that South Tyrol is almost entirely Catholic, and the clergy very anti-Italian, the Fascists have demanded that there be Italian sermons as well as German; they have had Italian priests and sisters appointed as heads of Catholic institutions such as orphan asylums and old people's homes, and they have kept a careful watch over priests who are reputed to be hostile. Furthermore, many of the societies of pre-war days—the Alpine Club, local volunteer fire brigades, music and choral clubs, etc.—have been dissolved for fear that they might become centers of opposition. As though this were not enough, direct action has been taken against individuals when other means have failed to break their antagonism.

From an economic point of view the creation of the frontier at the Brenner has been a hardship for South Tyrol. For instance, previous to 1919 great quantities of local wine were sold to Austria, but now this product has to compete with other Italian wines in the export trade, and cannot do so with great success. Formerly South Tyrol was one of the favorite tourist centers for Austrians and Germans, but now passport difficulties and the hostility of the Italians keep great numbers away. In other ways the new order has been an economic hardship. The Fascist authorities who have been placed in charge of local government have not hesitated to make large and unnecessary expenditures. For instance, the city of Bolzano was forced to pay 100,000 lire (about $5,500) toward a monument to the Italian victory. The expenditures of the towns have increased by leaps and bounds. Taxes jumped from 7,100,000 lire in 1922, to 16,657,405 in 1924. On the other hand, ambitious public works have been undertaken. A magnificent new station has been constructed at Bolzano; an attempt is being made to harness the vast amount of water power in the Alps by constructing great electrical plants; the railways are being electrified; land is being drained, etc. This work is directly connected with the policy of Italianization, however, for Italian workers are brought in to do the manual labor and are encouraged to settle among the Germans. The War Veterans Association has been especially active in furthering this movement, serving as an agency for finding homes for the colonizers, constructing large buildings for them at Bolzano, and undertaking great drainage projects to furnish labor for the newcomers. How many Italians have settled in South Tyrol cannot be stated, for no statistics have been published on the question, but their number is great enough to be a real factor in the campaign of Italianization.

The question which naturally follows a study of the methods of civic training employed in South Tyrol is: What have been the results? The answer is certain: The people of South Tyrol still remain hostile. In the elections of 1924 the Union of German Parties obtained 34,-983 votes as opposed to the Fascist party's 3,000.

South Tyrol has also been the subject of many international tilts. In the first years of Italian domination the statesmen of South Tyrol brought the problem before the International Parliamentary Union and other international organizations. In the last few years statesmen on both sides of the Alps have joined in the fray. On February 4, 1926, the president of the Council of Ministers in

Bavaria protested against the methods used to Italianize South Tyrol. Mussolini replied in bellicose terms:

In any case I declare with absolute certainty that Italy's policy in regard to South Tyrol will not be changed an iota. We shall introduce our laws in South Tyrol with cool forethought and in Fascist style. We shall make this territory Italian because it is Italian, Italian in its geographical and historical development. One can certainly maintain that the Brenner frontier was one of those boundaries drawn by the hand of God. The Germans in South Tyrol do not form a national minority but an ethnical residuum. I declare that there are only 180,000 Germans in South Tyrol, while in Czecho-Slovakia there are three and one-half million as opposed to only five million Czechs. I declare that of this 180,000 Germans of South Tyrol, 80,000 are Germanized Italians whom we shall win back and to whom we shall return their Italian names. . . . . The others are, above all, the remnants of barbarian invasions from a time when Italy was not a power but only a battlefield for other powers of the West and North. . . . . However, we say to the German people: we wish to live in friendship with you. Fascist Italy can, if necessary, carry the Tricolor further forward but never backward.

In 1928 a still more serious international crisis arose over South Tyrol. On February 23 the Austrian Parliament and the Austrian prime minister voiced their disapproval of the Italian domination in South Tyrol. This Mussolini took as a national insult and recalled the Italian minister to Vienna. Again Mussolini replied to the charges and ended with this declaration: "Hereby be it known to the Tyrolese, the Austrians and to the World, that all Italy with her living and with her dead is at the Brenner."[28] Although this crisis passed by, the Italian minister was sent back to Vienna, and Mussolini stated that "correct" international relations existed between Italy and Austria, South Tyrol remains a source of continual conflict between them.

[28] Speech to the Chamber, March 3, 1928.

6. *Fiume and Trieste.*—The national minority question confronts Italy not only in South Tyrol but also in the province of Venetia-Julia. This territory, which borders on the Adriatic from the province of Venice to Fiume and part of Dalmatia south of Fiume, was for years considered a part of *Italia irredenta.* By the Pact of London the Allies promised to cede the city of Trieste and its surroundings, the counties of Gorizia and Gradisca, and the cities of Zara and Sebenico in Dalmatia, several other towns, and a number of islands to Italy. At the Peace Conference there was great opposition to the fulfilment of these promises and, when it was known that they would not be granted and that Italy would not get Fiume, the adventurous poet d'Annunzio raised troops and occupied both Fiume and Zara. After long negotiations the Treaty of San Rapallo attempted to solve the situation by making Fiume an international port under the League of Nations and by ceding Zara to Italy. A settlement was made on these conditions which remained in force until after Mussolini came to power. A band of Fascists overthrew the helpless international government and consequently a new treaty was signed by Italy and Jugoslavia,[29] whereby Fiume was given to Italy in exchange for certain economic concessions.

The long narrow strip of territory, which reaches from the old 1914 frontier to Fiume and includes the city of Zara in Dalmatia, was not so Italian as had often been imagined by irredentists. The Austrian census of 1910 showed that of 928,401 people in Venetia-Julia, 326,715 were Slovenes, 140,240 Croats, and 5,622 Germans. On the whole, the population in the cities is Italian, whereas a large percentage of the rural population is Slav. Italy was at once faced with an important national minority

[29] Accord of Rome, signed January 27, 1924.

and on the whole has followed the policy pursued in South Tyrol. During the first few years some cultural leniency was displayed but with the coming of the Fascists all was changed. Mussolini had always been interested in the question, had visited d'Annunzio after the march on Fiume, and had lauded the poet in his *Popolo d'Italia*. He favored a severe policy of Italianization and no sooner had he seized the reins of government than he choked the opposition press, made the schools Italian, sent young Slav men to Italy for military service, dissolved Slav societies, and severely punished anyone who dared oppose the Régime. In this policy he has been aided by the Italians in the cities, for strong *fasci* have been established in the largest centers. The one at Trieste has played an exceptionally important rôle.

There has been a strong current of discontent among the Slav population. In the elections of 1921 the political party of Slavs in the province of Venetia-Julia obtained 48,784 votes (33.6 per cent of the total) and elected 5 of the 16 deputies. After the advent of Fascism this proportion was somewhat reduced, for in the elections of 1924 the Slavs obtained 29,847 "valid" votes (11.1 per cent of the total), the Fascist party having made great gains. Most of the opposition can be traced directly to nationalist causes although some of it is undoubtedly economic, for the ports of Fiume and Trieste have suffered greatly in being cut off from their hinterland. For instance, the traffic in the port of Fiume, which was 22½ million hundredweight in 1913, was only 2 million in 1923, and 4 in 1924.[30]

[30] Speech by Mussolini, January 22, 1925.

CHAPTER III

INTERNATIONAL RELATIONS

1. *The Peace of Versailles.*—Fascism was born of interventionism, of eagerness to join the great fray. Even before the war, Mussolini had been an anti-Austria propagandist in the Trentino, and his defection from the Socialist party at the outbreak of the war, leading him at first to a denunciation of the Triple Alliance and then to an active propaganda in favor of intervention on the side of the Entente, was an influential factor in pushing Italy into the war. The "humiliation" of Versailles, coming immediately after Italy's elation over victory, merely increased the general disillusionment in Italy after the war, and the general bitterness against those who had pushed the nation into so fruitless a sacrifice. It was in defense of its war policy, therefore, that Fascism rearose in 1919, a "post-war interventionism."

Defense of the war and denunciation of the Peace of Versailles were practically the only policies the various brands of early Fascism had in common toward a united platform. On internal issues the Fascists were hopelessly divided; some were Republicans, others Monarchists; some Socialists, others Liberals; some Syndicalists, others the most reactionary bourgeois Nationalists. Consequently the Fascist politicians from 1919 to the present, have preached the glories of the war, the vindication of its sacrifices, and an aggressive nationalistic foreign policy as the keynote of Fascism. Certainly in Mussolini's own mind the problems of foreign policy were uppermost, and one reason for his turning so savagely on the opposition parties was that they distracted his attention and efforts from foreign affairs.

This being the case, ex-members of the Nationalist party have been the backbone of the Fascist government, for this party, above all others, has made foreign policy its prime concern. Enrico Corradini, one of the founders of the Nationalist Association in 1909, is still active in the cause and is vigorously co-operating with the Fascist Ré-gime. D'Annunzio is still the Nationalist hero par excel-lence. But the most important leaders at present are two younger Nationalists, Luigi Federzoni and Francesco Coppola. Federzoni is the politician, and Coppola the journalist, of nationalistic foreign policy. A good idea of Fascist nationalism in foreign affairs can be obtained by reading *La Politica*. This political journal was founded in 1918, during the height of the internal crisis, by Cop-pola and Alfredo Rocco, with the express purpose of arousing public opinion to an interest in foreign affairs.[1] Among the other Nationalists who are active in the Fas-cist ranks should be mentioned Dino Grandi, Forges-Davanzati, Cantalupo, and Maraviglia. These men were hardly less violent in their attack on Italy's post-war gov-ernments than were the Communists. Nationalism from 1918 to 1922 was of a decidedly revolutionary character; it joined the general chorus of "Down with the govern-ment!" Of course, it gave reasons exactly opposite to those of the Socialists. The government, especially under Giolitti, realizing that it could please neither Socialists nor Nationalists, finally allowed the two disgruntled ele-ments to fight it out between them. And then, national-ism, having defeated socialism, turned on the government. Since the March on Rome nationalist statesmanship and

[1] Cf. Schneider, *Making the Fascist State*, pp. 24–25.

imperialist philosophy have completely dominated foreign policy.

The first objects of Fascist attack were naturally the
Peace of Versailles and the Allies who were responsible
for Italy's diplomatic defeat. President Wilson was wor-
shiped as a hero for a few days, and then denounced as
the worst of all the Versailles villains, because of his ob-
stinate stand on Fiume and his rejection of the London
treaties. But the Italian wrath soon included England
and France on the theory that these two nations were trying to conceal their own imperialistic ambitions behind
President Wilson, and that they were making away with
the lion's share while they set the whole world gaping at
the League of Nations.

2. *The League of Nations and internationalism.*—
The League became the second object of Fascist scorn.
The Italian nationalists regard it not merely as an impo-
tent and sentimental lip-service to internationalism but
as positively obnoxious and dangerous for the following
reasons:

(1) The League is dominated by England and
France and serves to perpetuate their power and prestige in international affairs: It, therefore, not only in-
sures the status quo of the "plutocratic nations," but also
gives them a convenient instrument for meddling in the
affairs of all smaller countries.

(2) The League is interested merely in maintaining
the status quo, especially territorial boundaries and colonial holdings, while Italy is frankly dissatisfied with
the status quo and is bending her diplomatic efforts to
change it.

(3) The League erects a false internationalistic ideology to screen still dominant imperialistic politics: The
denunciation of this contrast between theory and fact,

and the resulting hypocrisy, self-deception, and dishonesty, is one of the favorite occupations of Italian nationalist journalism.

The same general criticism is applied to the American disarmament policy and the Kellogg treaties. They are regarded as cheap and hypocritical measures to perpetuate the present favorable status quo of the United States. Fascism, on the contrary, is frankly military in spirit and willing to test its fighting strength. War is generally referred to as a "probable event" and Mussolini even suggested that the crisis may come sometime between 1935 and 1940, though he later modified his statement, saying that the crisis would not necessarily take the form of war.[2]

Naturally, if the foregoing represents the real opinion of the Fascist government on international relations, other nations regard Italy's participation in the League, the Washington agreements, and the Kellogg treaties as hypocritical. In fact, even in Italy there were not a few who urged withdrawal from the League at the time when Spain withdrew. The official explanation of Italy's continued participation in international politics is that, in the first place, Italy wants to give every possible proof of a sincere devotion to peace and to an even more radical removal of the causes of war; and, in the second place, Italy's only chance of asserting her rights and checking the "plutocratic" ambitions of her more wealthy and powerful neighbors is through the machinery of the League. Consequently the Fascist government has taken every possible opportunity of enhancing its prestige among international bodies and making its power felt at Geneva. It has been especially active in weaning the Geneva Labor Bureau from socialist and Russian influences, in advertising Fascist economic policy at the Geneva Econom-

[2] See speech of Mussolini in the Chamber, May 26, 1927.

ic Congress, in counter-attacking anti-Fascist emigrés
who have tried to use the League for their propaganda,
and in aiding various international institutes of a social
nature, such as the Agricultural Bureau, the codification
of private law, social relief, and educational motion pictures.

There are at least two agencies through which Fascism is trying to make headway for itself among international circles. One is the Institute for International
Intellectual Co-operation, affiliated with the League of
Nations. Its office in Paris (especially the propaganda
division under Giuseppe Prezzolini) is a center of contact between Fascist and French intellectual and political circles. Another branch is now being established at
Rome. Recently a Centre international d'études sur le
fascisme (Cinef) was founded, with headquarters at
Lausanne. It is professedly not devoted to propaganda
but to the scholarly "documentation" of Fascism. Nevertheless, it serves to present Fascism as a movement of
international scope and universal historical and political
importance. Three of its leading spirits, H. de Vries de
Heekelingen, J. S. Barnes, and Homem Christo, are notorious Fascist enthusiasts, and at least half of the articles in the first volume published by the Cinef were typically Fascist, having been written by prominent Fascist
politicians in Italy. On the whole, however, Fascism is
content to be merely Italian, and though its theories are
conceived in universal terms, its politics is limited to
Italy.

3. *Italy and the Great Powers.*—Fascist foreign policy toward the Great Powers has been rather tortuous.
At first, under the disillusionment of the Versailles
Treaty, the burden of the war debt, and resentment over
the immigration barriers of the United States, the gener-

al spirit of Fascism was hostile toward "the Anglo-Saxon world." Mussolini once suggested that Italy must turn eastward, to Russia, for help against the imperialisms of the Western world. England was to be forced out of the Mediterranean and Italy was to develop a huge merchant marine, to compete with England for the carrying trade with the East and develop commerce with South America.[3] But after a few diplomatic skirmishes with England, culminating in the Corfu affair, relations changed. The Locarno Conference and subsequent friendly encounters between Chamberlain and Mussolini gave the Fascist imagination a different turn. England and Italy would co-operate to keep peace between France and Germany! Differences with Great Britain were soon patched up—Italy agreed to keep hands off Turkey and Egypt, and in return she received from England some additions to her African possessions. Since then Italy has regarded Great Britain as a big brother, and her foreign policy has taken on an English color.

France is the chief object of attack now. Italian nationalists have no faith in a rapprochement between France and Germany.[4] Germany, they think, is bound to take revenge as soon as she is able and then Italy will "follow her own interests." The nationalists have been persistently emphasizing the divergence between French and Italian interests and relations are certainly not becoming more friendly. Some of the imperialistic extremists even urged a military alliance with Germany. The chief sources of friction between France and Italy are the following:

(1) Nice and Corsica, and French policy during the *risorgimento,* though not serious sore spots, are, however,

[3] See *Popolo d'Italia* for 1919.

[4] Cf. Andrea Torre in *Civiltà Fascista* (Rome, 1928).

old grievances which Italy has and which she can revive whenever opportune.

(2) Tunis is a serious problem. Italian "Africanists" can never forgive their government for not going into Tunis ahead of the French government. The large Italian population in Tunis is a constant source of friction, since the Italians demand larger national rights and privileges than the French are willing to concede.

(3) Italy thinks she, rather than France, ought to have Syria, or its equivalent.

(4) Italy demands the right to participate in all international settlements affecting the Mediterranean, and finally secured such recognition at the Tangiers Conference, despite French opposition.

(5) The French policy of upholding the Little Entente is directly opposed to the Italian policy.[5]

(6) There were innumerable jealousies and dislikes generated between the French and Italian troops during the War.

(7) France receives large numbers of Italian immigrants (over 132,000 annually), who are somewhat readily absorbed into the French nation: Italy now wants national "cultural" protection for Italians in France.

(8) French hospitality to anti-Fascists aroused indignation among the Fascists, especially at the time of the attacks on Mussolini's life.

Despite these divergent interests, relations have improved lately between the two countries; France yielded in the Tangiers dispute, and in addition took the initiative in carrying on diplomatic conversations and framing a *modus vivendi*. Italy co-operated in this attempt at conciliation by keeping the delicate issues of the Little Entente and the Balkans out of the discussion.

[5] See Schneider: *Making the Fascist State*, ch. I.

4. *The Little Entente and the Balkans.*—The focus of Fascist foreign policy has been Jugoslavia. Almost every move which Italy has made is aimed directly or indirectly at isolating her Slav neighbor and thwarting Jugoslav prestige and ambitions in the Balkans. First of all, the Little Entente must be broken, if possible, and France detached from he: patronage of this group of nations.

Relations with Jugoslavia center about two major problems, the Italian cities in Dalmatia and the rivalry between Jugoslavia (backed by France) and Italy for hegemony in the Balkans. The first problem was approached in the negotiations of Nettuno, which provided for considerable economic and cultural privileges for Italians in Dalmatia. This, of course, did not satisfy the irredentist nationalists who insist on the annexation of Dalmatia and on regarding the Adriatic as an "internal Italian sea," but it was all that could be hoped for under present political conditions.

The Treaty of Nettuno was negotiated on the part of Jugoslavia by Nincic, who wanted friendship with Italy presumably as a necessary preliminary to the establishment of a Balkan hegemony for Jugoslavia, but his policy received such opposition in the Jugoslav Parliament that ratification of the treaty was delayed several years and aroused widespread popular indignation against Italy. Italy promptly poured oil on this conflagration by recognizing the independence of Albania with great ceremony, and by negotiating a military alliance (the Treaty of Tirana, signed November 27, 1926), thus virtually establishing a protectorate in Albania. This was a direct blow to Nincic's Balkan policy. He resigned immediately and an anti-Italian government came into power. By various diplomatic maneuvers and treaties Hungary and Bulgaria have been befriended by Italy.

Officially, of course, the sole object of all these treaties has been to establish definite and peaceful working relations with as many states as possible, and to treat the Balkan states as sovereign units to be protected from each other's ambitions. If it were difficult to read between the lines, a little reading of the Fascist press would make all clear. Italian papers were not only allowed extraordinary liberty in publishing detailed accounts of Jugoslav attacks on Italian foreign policy, but featured in the headlines, editorials, and political speeches the hostile "incidents" and "Italophobia." France, too, was included in the attack. In short, the press was obviously encouraged to make the most of the friction.

5. *Colonial policy and eastward expansion.*—At the same time that Mussolini has been carrying on this irredentist Adriatic policy, Federzoni and others have been pushing a vigorous African colonial policy. Several rebellions in Cyrenaica and Southern Tripolitania were speedily crushed and serious efforts applied to the economic development of the colonies. By means of colonial expositions, excursions, celebrations, movies, and literature of all sorts, a popular interest in the colonies, especially in Tripoli, has been stimulated. The natives, who had been granted some liberties by the Liberal régime after the war, were put under a strict Fascist discipline and a more or less military government. Extensive projects for the economic exploitation and commercial development of all the colonies are under way, especially the harbor of Bangasi and the valley of the Juba in Somalia.

In addition to this attention to her own colonies, Italy has been eager to make her influence felt among the Islamic states in general. The treaties with Yemen and

Persia, and similar diplomatic moves, are aimed at promoting Italian commercial expansion and diplomatic prestige all along the Red Sea route.[6]

6. *Mare Nostrum and the new Roman empire.*— These endeavors are symptoms of the Fascist imperial ambition to make Italy supreme in the Mediterranean. Other moves in this direction were: the treaty with Spain, which was obviously aimed against French influence on the Mediterranean; Italy's insistence on being represented at the Tangiers Conference on the ground that she was a "great Mediterranean power," and the definite annexation of Rhodes and the Dodecanese Islands.

A wildly exuberant imperialistic theory accompanies these practical achievements. The talk of the new Roman empire is a commonplace by this time, and it is supplemented by the revival of Gioberti's theory of the "moral primacy of Italy" in the world. Another phase of Italy's imperial caliber and destiny is her vigorous birthrate and "demographic energy." Another is her "spiritual imperialism," that is, her traditional leadership in art, science, and civilization in general. Anglo-Saxons are to this day frequently regarded as barbarians not yet sufficiently permeated with the civilizing graces of the Italic stock. The Catholic church is Roman religious imperialism. And, lastly, the achievements of Italian labor the world over are heralded as "proletarian or poor man's imperialism."

7. *Foreign Fasci.*—A distinctly Fascist creation in the realm of foreign policy is the organization of the foreign *fasci*. Until recently these have sprung up rather sporadically all over the world under the influence of local enthusiasm and unofficial organizers. Now they are being brought directly under the central control of the

[6] See Roberto Cantalupo, *Italia Musulmana.*

party. The following constitution for foreign *fasci,* published in February, 1928, will give the reader an idea of the organization, aims, and activities of these *fasci.*

ARTICLE 1

Foreign *fasci* are the organizations of Italians residing abroad who have chosen obedience to the *Duce* and the Law of Fascism as a rule to govern their private and civic life, and whose aim it is to gather the colonies of Italians living in foreign lands around the symbol of the Lictor's Rods.

The commandments issued by the *Duce* as a daily guide to Fascists living abroad are the following.

1. Fascists living abroad must obey the laws of the country which has given them hospitality. They must give daily proof of this obedience and, if necessary, be an example to the citizens themselves.

2. They should not participate in the internal politics of the countries in which they reside.

3. They should not arouse factional quarrels in their colonies but should rather settle them in the shadow of the Lictor's Rods.

4. They should be exemplary in public and private honesty.

5. They should respect the representatives of Italy abroad and obey their directions and instructions.

6. They should defend Italianism of the past and of the present.

7. They should give assistance to needy Italians.

8. They should be disciplined abroad, even as Italians at home are disciplined.

ARTICLE 2

The organs of the foreign *fasci* are:

1. The General Secretariat with headquarters at Rome.

2. The foreign *fasci.*

ARTICLE 3

In connection with every *fascio* there shall be established a section of the Advance Guard and of the *Balilla,* and a Feminine *fascio.*

The foreign *fasci* are directly dependent on the General Secretary.

The General Secretary may group the *fasci* in a single consular district if necessary. In this case, the secretary of the *fascio* of the chief city in the consular district is also as a rule the secretary of the zone.

ARTICLE 4

The secretary of the zone is nominated by the General Secretary.

ARTICLE 5

The secretary of the *fascio,* nominated directly by the General Secretary has charge of the management of the *fascio.*

ARTICLE 6

The essential task of the *fasci* is the assistance of fellow-countrymen abroad. The secretary of the *fascio* will explain the implications of this task to the representatives of the Fascist State (the Consul-General, Consul, and Vice-Consul), coöperating with them in their undertakings and daily work.

ARTICLES 7–10

(Details of administration.)

ARTICLE 11

The General Secretary of the foreign *fasci* shall have the power to apply immediately and without further procedure the various disciplinary punishments with respect to those officers or members who are found guilty (*a*) of exciting discord among the *fasci* or in the Italian colonies, or (*b*) of disobeying consular authorities or diminishing their prestige before other Italians and before foreigners.

ARTICLE 12

The General Secretary is authorized to prescribe rules for the internal operation of the organizations.

As can readily be seen, the chief purpose of this constitution is to get the Fascists under control in order to prevent conflicts between Fascists and anti-Fascists in foreign countries, which have heretofore caused considerable embarrassment, and in order to strengthen the authority of the consuls over irresponsible Fascists. This action is really a supplement to a general reform of the diplomatic corps which has been undertaken in the interests of centralizing responsibility and co-ordinating all Italian foreign activities, "cultural" as well as political.

8. *Cultural expansion and emigration.*—Reduction of the stream of emigration has practically been forced on Italy by other powers, but this fact has merely encouraged the general Fascist policy of replacing indiscriminate emigration with constructive colonization. Colonization may take place either in Italy's own colonies or oftener in foreign countries, where Italian immigrants are to be regarded still as Italian citizens,[7] and hence are to be organized into solid cultural groups in which Italian nationality can be better preserved.

The foreign *fasci,* just described, constitute one means of promoting this "spiritual imperialism." Another is the patriotic society Dante Alighieri,[8] which was founded in 1889 for the purpose of "diffusing the Italian language and Italian culture abroad and holding high the sentiment of Italian nationalism—above every party and every class."[9] Its usual methods are the founding of local branches, schools, and libraries. The Dante Alighieri maintains schools in 25 cities in Europe, 15 in Africa, 19 in North and South America, and 1 in Asia. It has libraries or local branches in 104 of the world's cities and sends books to libraries in 42 others. It also offers a number of prizes to elementary school children for excellence in the study of the Italian language. An idea of the importance of this society may be gathered from its membership, which has grown from 2,000 in 1892 to 78,347 in 1926.

Of a more technical nature is the Fascist Colonial Institute (formerly the Italian Colonial Institute), which was founded in 1908.[10] It aims to form and develop an Italian colonial consciousness and study questions con-

[7] Of course, as Mussolini explicitly stated, this does not apply to naturalized citizens of other countries. It is intended, however, to prevent a too easy absorption of Italians by foreign nations.

[8] Headquarters: Via Aracoeli 3, Rome. Organ: *Le Pagine della Dante* (bimonthly).

[9] Art. 1 of the Constitution.   [10] Headquarters: Via Giustiani 5, Rome.

cerning Italian possessions and districts which may become colonies. Its propaganda is carried on by branch societies, by the colonial publication, *L'Altremare* (edited by the Nationalist Roberto Cantalupo and sent to all its members), by a colonial annual, by the institution of courses on colonial subjects in schools, by lectures, etc. This society has been taken into the Fascist fold and recognized by the party as the sole agent for colonial propaganda in Italy.

Other means of encouraging interest in the expansion of Italy are described in the following excerpt from Mussolini's address on foreign affairs to the Senate, June 5, 1928.

Another organization very recently established is the Committee for the Diffusion of Italian Culture Abroad. The diffusion of culture abroad is certainly a durable and efficacious means of penetration. But too many institutions, too many agencies, societies and organizations, public and private, in Italy and abroad, have dedicated themselves to this task, almost always with inadequate means. Hence their efforts have too often either ended fruitlessly or, worse still, counteracted each other. The new Committee must study the means necessary to coördinate and give useful direction to the various enterprises and will be provided with a permanent office for carrying on precisely this work. In the meantime the General Directors of Italian Schools abroad have continued their activity: 100 new teachers; new elementary schools in Algeria, Argentina, Bulgaria, Brazil, Chile, Egypt, France, Germany, England, Morocco, Peru, Poland, Rumania, Switzerland and Uruguay; new secondary and high schools in Athens, Bayreut, Corfu, Philippopoli, Port Said, Rosario and Tangiers, with an increase of about 6,000 students in the academic population of our schools abroad, a large part of them being of foreign nationalities; new chairs and lectureships of Italian language and literature at the Universities of Prague, Bucharest, Cluy, Warsaw, Cracow, Budapest, Marseilles and Coimbra. These are the comforting fruits of this work.

Another novelty is the Bulletin of the Ministry of Foreign Affairs, which has been revived and is to be added to the other publications edited by the Ministry of Foreign Affairs—*La Rassegna della Stampa Estera* and *La Rassegna delle Riviste Estere*—which already have a wide circulation and are very useful for any one who wishes to know the opinions expressed in the press of the world on the subject of Italy and on great international problems.

The Bulletin of the Ministry of Foreign Affairs, with which the former Bulletin of Emigration has been fused, consists of five parts. The second, third, fourth and fifth parts contain laws and decrees, treaties, international conventions and agreements, etc. . . . . In the first part every month the most important events and acts of the Government and Régime are recorded and these will be explained and commented upon by the consuls even in the remotest Italian nuclei in all parts of the world.

But the organic reform of major importance is the discontinuance of the General Commissariat of Emigration which was so numerous in personnel and offices as to constitute a veritable Ministry. The General Directorate of Italians Abroad . . . . will consist of a total of only seven offices, including those it has taken over which were already attached to the Ministry of Foreign Affairs.

The General Directorate of Italians Abroad will not limit its functions to official and administrative assistance for emigrants. Above all this last term is tending to disappear from the Italian vocabulary. There is no longer the emigrant on the one hand and the citizen on the other. Always and everywhere, rich or poor, manual laborer or intellectual or tourist, there is the Italian *citizen*. Equal rights, equal duties. I have given instructions to abolish the emigrants' passport, which used to accompany the worker who was lacking in means or fortune, as much as to say that he was not yet an adult, and have provided that for all citizens indiscriminately a new and uniform type of passport be issued.

The honest Italian, faithful to the Régime, has the right to hold his head high with pride both at home and abroad, whatever be his social condition. . . . .

There can be no technical and philanthropic care for Italian communities abroad without political care. And vice versa. A single aim in a single organism, and at its center the Ministry of Foreign Affairs. Single and indivisible are the tasks and responsibilities of him who represents the sovereignty of the state among the Italian groups abroad—the Consul. From the official duties which concern the individual to the great displays of the group as a whole, there is an enormous work which must proceed thoughtfully, organically, passionately and tenaciously—a work of protection and defense of the Italian people and its traditions.

CHAPTER IV

FASCISM AND CATHOLICISM

1. *Fascist philosophy of religion.*—The attitude of Fascism toward religion is still quite flexible. Two general factors serve to explain this fact: one is the notorious pragmatic ability of Fascist ideas to change with changing practical problems; the other is the varied heritage which the various groups composing Fascism have brought with them and which has not yet been "synthesized." (*a*) The socialistic, republican, and futuristic elements, represented by the Mussolini-Marinetti Fascism of 1919, were violently anticlerical and even anti-Christian. Mussolini in his early days outdid Marinetti in his attacks on all religious institutions and as late as 1920 proclaimed that the church would be one of the first victims of the Fascist Revolution. (*b*) The Nationalists, on the other hand, were Catholic modernists, and recognized the church as one of the essential and traditional forms of national culture. D'Annunzio and his schools had led many to a neopaganism and to the cult of ancient Rome, but most of the Nationalists, and recently d'Annunzio himself, recognized the Catholic church as essentially Roman and imperialistic and, hence, as Italian. The church's repudiation of nationalism and modernism erected an intellectual barrier but did not prevent a political friendship; in fact, the recent hostilities between the church and the Action Française were applauded in certain Nationalist circles as helping the cause of Italian Catholicism. (*c*) Still another distinctive attitude toward the Catholic religion came from the idealists of the school of Croce and

Gentile. This school of philosophy rejects not merely orthodox Catholicism but also Catholic modernism, and regards true religion as something more universal than any one church, and welcomes the multiplicity of particular religions as particular aspects of the universal spirit. Furthermore it regards religion in general as but one among several forms of the spiritual life, placing it on a level with science, art, and other civilized institutions. The Fascist idealists, following Gentile rather than Croce, insist that the national state is the supreme synthesis of the spiritual life and that, therefore, religion must be subordinated to it. Consequently they reject anticlericalism, on the one hand, and, on the other, they reject the politics of Cavour based on "a free Church in a free State." The basis of religion, according to them, is the immanent and historical union between God and the nation,[1] of which the church is but an external expression. Any religion is real in so far as it actually lives and functions in the mind and tradition of the people; in Italy this happens to be the Catholic religion. The idealists themselves, personally, have "transcended" Catholicism and Christianity, and believe in idealism as the culmination of religious enlightenment; but in so far as they are *Italian* idealists they must know and share the religious and spiritual life of their people.

In the face of these various philosophies of religion it is idle to try to commit Fascism as a whole to any one of them. About all that can be said is that the nationalist ideas are most current among Fascist politicians and most congenial to the practical policy of the Régime. Mussolini's recent expressions on the subject of religion show that he has adopted the nationalist position, except that he is, if anything, more orthodox. The one point on

[1] Cf. Mazzini's formula, *Dio e popolo*.

which all seem to agree, and the only point which much matters, is that religion is an essential element of national life and, therefore, cannot be ignored by the state but must be incorporated in the state. The Italian *people* is Catholic and its church must, therefore, be respected; the government must be as Catholic as the church and, if possible, more so.

2. *Fascist religious policy.*—The practical evidence of this attitude toward religion was Gentile's school reform.[2] For educational purposes religion is treated exactly as science, art, or business. The child begins with the commonplaces of worship, dogma, and mythology, until he becomes familiar with the religious life of the people. Since the teachers are supposed to be Italian enough to know the elements of the Catholic religion, this early religious instruction is intrusted to them and not to religious professionals. In the secondary schools and universities this instruction gradually becomes more critical, as the student learns more of the intricacies of his national culture and takes part in its intellectual traditions, until religion culminates in philosophy. At least, this is Gentile's idea; for he makes a basic distinction between religious education and Catholic training, and in his mind the school reform was the beginning of the end of the church's monopoly over the religious life of the people: the state was to have its innings. In every schoolroom there must be a crucifix, but it is invariably placed under a big portrait of the king! Gentile's successors in the Ministry of Education, however, have adopted a more superficial policy. They have catered to the church, by allowing it a fairly free hand in selecting the textbooks on religion, by introducing more orthodox religious education in the secondary schools, and by encouraging Cath-

[2] See chap. v.

olic universities. They have not yet yielded to the church's request for admission into the state universities but, on the whole, they are much more willing to turn over religious education to the church than were the idealists who instigated the reform.

The Fascist reform of the Penal Code embodies many Catholic features. Divorce is abolished, antibirth-control measures are adopted, cabarets have been closed, swearing is made a crime, and respect for the church and its institutions is legally enforced.

The salaries of priests and higher clergy have been raised considerably by state decree and their privileges have been extended.

One of the greatest favors which Fascism performed for the church was the destruction of Freemasonry. Of course the government had its own political reasons. The prominent part taken by Masons in opposition tactics, ranging from a generous and international support of the Parliamentary opposition to the implication of General Capello and the grand-master, Torrigiani, in the attempted assassination of Mussolini, gives the Fascists abundant cause for hating Freemasonry. There has been political opposition to Masonic tactics for many years in Italy, even among anticlericals, and during the war the Grand Orient made itself especially odious by its dubious war attitude. On February 15, 1923, the Grand Council of the Fascist party passed the following resolution:

Inasmuch as recent political events and certain attitudes and votes of Freemasonry give rise to a well-grounded suspicion that Freemasonry is pursuing policies and adopting methods opposed to those of Fascism, the Grand Council asks Fascists who are Masons to choose between belonging to the National Fascist Party and belonging to Freemasonry, since there can be but one set of discipline for Fascists, namely, the discipline of Fascism; but one hierarchy—that of Fascism; and but one obedience—absolute, devoted and daily obedience to the Head and leaders of Fascism.

Of the dozen Masons who were members of the Council, eight voted for the resolution. In certain circles this action was not taken very seriously, being interpreted as an indirect move on the part of the Scottish Rite, to which many Fascists belonged, to destroy its larger rival, the Grand Orient. But all doubts as to the thoroughness of Fascism's attack on Freemasonry were dispelled in 1925, when all secret societies were abolished in Italy. The church officially congratulated the government on this move.[3]

Further testimony of the state's hospitality to religion is given in the cordial relations which are being established between local Fascist politicians and priests and prelates. Church celebrations are morally supported and ostentatiously attended by the civil authorities, and vice versa the ecclesiastical hierarchy takes part in civic functions. Chaplains have been reinstated in the army, military monuments and processions are frequently blessed by bishops, and new works of the Régime are usually dedicated with an accompaniment of religious rites. Everything is done to make religious rites appear as a phase of the political life of the nation. There is, of course, occasional friction, and during Fascism's early stages the friction was often acute. The most serious recent "incident" between church and state (apart from the Balilla issue, which we shall discuss later) was the church's intervention in behalf of the German churches in the Italian Tyrol. This move was resented by the Fascist press, which accused the church of being an instrument of foreign meddling in Italian affairs; the government was unyielding, and replied by further restrictions on Catholic children's organizations. But on the whole there is a growing genial mutual respect between officers of church and

---

[3] See chapter on Italian Freemasonry in Maurice Vaussard, *Sur la nouvelle Italie* (Paris: Librairie Valois, 1928).

state. This cordiality in the rank and file of both church and state may in the near future lead to still greater cordiality between the papal court and the government. A manifestation of this feeling of rapprochement came in 1927 when, with great ceremony, in the presence of the queen of Italy and many high dignitaries of church and state, a large cross was erected in the Colosseum. A flock of white doves encircled the scene. The theme of imperial Rome and the Roman church was widely celebrated in the press. One noted writer summed it up: *Da Roma la croce il mondo salvo.*

3. *Church and state: the Roman question.*—This growing friendliness between church and state in general led to rumors concerning a settlement of the vexing "Roman question," the problem of the recognition of the temporal authority of the papacy. This question was debated about once a year. The leaders of the debate were usually the papers, *Il Popolo d'Italia* and *L'Osservatore Romano,* which are practically official organs of state and church, respectively. One occasion of this debate was the huge oecumenical congress at Bologna in September, 1927. Arnaldo Mussolini, editor of *Il Popolo d'Italia,* noted the contrast between the triumphal Fascist celebration a year previously in the same great stadium and the Catholic celebration at the congress—the contrast between the medieval and the modern world, and he suggested that the issue was really up to the church in that a settlement of the question awaited the church's willingness to recognize the sovereignty of the state in this modern world. Gentile entered the debate by defending the status quo and suggesting that nothing would be gained for Fascism by "solving" the Roman question. The *Osservatore Romano* and various Catholic writers replied: (1) that the church can never accept the Fascist political

philosophy which assigns to it a subordinate position *within* the state, because religion is the supreme form of the spiritual life and the church is, therefore, morally obligated to assert its primacy; (2) that the church is a universal and supernatural, not a national, institution; (3) that the Roman question could be settled if the Italian government would agree to treat with the papal court as *pares inter pares,* and not as a recipient of state charity; (4) that the pope does not need land but must receive formal recognition as the spiritual "father" of the Italian people.

Rumors of an approaching settlement spread rapidly; the church was reported as willing to waive territorial claims and accept the money indemnity offered by the Italian government, but hitherto always refused, and the government was reported as willing to recognize the "spiritual authority" of the church. Nevertheless the incident was closed as far as the public was concerned by the following official statement in the Fascist *Foglio d'Ordini,* of October 20, 1927:

The debate between the spokesmen of the Holy See and several Fascist writers admits, for the time being, of the following conclusions:

(1) The conduct of the debate has been elevated and calm, worthy of the delicacy of the question at issue and consonant with the new atmosphere created by the Fascist Régime.

(2) It may be said, on the basis of the articles in the *Osservatore Romano,* that the Vatican does not regard the problem as an international one, but as simply involving two parties, the Italian State and the Holy See. This is just, both historically and logically, and it avoids dangerous interventions and useless complications.

(3) It seems legitimate to infer from the text of several articles in the *Osservatore Romano* that the question of the real political and legal independence of the Holy See is not necessarily bound up with territorial considerations. It is obvious that for Fascist Italy there is not, and cannot be, any question of a restoration even in the slightest

degree of the Temporal Power ended in 1870, to the immeasurable
advantage (in our opinion) of the Church of Rome's moral prestige.

In the face of these current developments Fascists who are really
aware of the power and nature of the Fascist State should avoid both
of two antithetical positions, either of which is far from the truth:
the position of those who dogmatically assert that the Roman Question cannot possibly be solved, and the position of those who believe
the Question can be easily and speedily solved.

History has known no knot too difficult to untie by force, by pa-
tience, or by prudence; so it is with the Roman Question. The Fascist
Régime has the whole twentieth century before it and can succeed
where democratic liberalism has repeatedly failed, without abdicating
to anyone the fundamental rights of the State.

The conclusion may well be: difficult, but not impossible.

It was not impossible, as events have since proved. In
January, 1929, rumors suggested that negotiations between the church and the state were under way and that
they would probably result in a successful settlement.
The rumors were not false. February 6 Pope Pius XI
announced that an agreement had been reached, and on
February 11 Cardinal Gasparri and Premier Mussolini
signed a treaty which put an end to the ambiguous relations between the church and the Italian state.

The agreement was composed of two parts: a political treaty and a concordat. According to the terms of the
treaty the papal domain, slightly extended to include St.
Peter's Square, was declared an independent state to be
known as Vatican City, entitled to all the rights and im-
munities of a sovereign power. The state reaffirmed that
Catholicism was the state religion of Italy; promised that
all propaganda against the pope or attempts on his life
would be punished in the same fashion as similar action
against the king; recognized the church's claim to extra-
territoriality rights in several of the church's holdings in
Rome; renounced its right to tax contributions for the
support of the church or ecclesiastics, and agreed to pay

the Holy See an indemnity of a nominal value of 2,000,-000,000 lire ($105,000,000) for losses suffered on account of the unification of Italy. The actual value of the indemnity was reduced because half of it was to be paid at once in interest-bearing state securities which were not at par. The balance was to be paid in ten equal annual instalments. For its part the Holy See declared the Roman question definitely settled and recognized the "Kingdom of Italy under the dynasty of the House of Savoy, with Rome as capital of the Italian State."

The concordat specified the relations between the church and Italy. It began by declaring the church to be free in the exercise of its cult—"a free church in a free state," at least in theory. As far as the clergy were concerned the state agreed not to tax their salaries, or to require military service of them, and to provide separate prisons for them in case of condemnation for crimes. The state promised to recognize certain religious holidays (which it had already actually done), while the church reciprocated by agreeing to have prayers said on these days for the king and the Italian state. In order that the state might protect itself from possible antagonism from the higher clergy, provision was made that archbishops, bishops, and coadjutors might not be appointed without the approval of the state, and that they might not assume the rights of office without swearing allegiance to Italy. In fact, all persons enjoying ecclesiastical benefices must be approved by the government and must be of Italian nationality. The state went still further and suggested that bishops and parochial priests know the Italian language, although the possibility of having subordinates who know the local language is clearly recognized.

The church, on the other hand, received decided advantages for these concessions. Religious orders and congregations were made legal bodies, capable of owning property; the state surrendered its right to place a special tax on property in the hands of religious bodies, and recognized the legality of religious marriages, a thing that it had not done previously. Of still greater importance was the pledge made by the state to continue its present policy of compulsory religious education in elementary schools and from the date of the ratification of the accord to place this instruction only in the hands of teachers approved by ecclesiastical officials. It even went further and stated that it considered religious instruction to be the fulcrum of public education and agreed to develop it in secondary schools.

The spirit of conciliation which is so apparent throughout the concordat is well illustrated by Article XLIII. In this section the state recognized the Azione Cattolica Italiana on the promise that it refrain from politics, and the church took the "opportunity" to reiterate its order to ecclesiastics to refrain from enrolling or participating in party politics. In such a way have church and state struck a friendly working agreement.

No sooner had the terms of the treaty leaked out than speculation was rife concerning their practical significance. Although the future alone can reveal what the results may be, certain effects seem approximately sure. For instance, Italian Catholics, who have had their tempers ruffled only too often during the Fascist régime, will undoubtedly feel more friendly toward the existing order and show a greater willingness to support it than formerly. This tendency was indicated by an almost immediate change in the tone of the *Osservatore Romano* following the signing of the pact. This spirit of rapprochement will also have its repercussions among foreign Catholics. On March 9 the pope himself made a statement to the effect that all the Catholic world approved the accord, an approval which, in many cases, will be extended to include the ruling powers in Italy. Hence, it would seem that Fascism has strengthened its position by the agreement.

For its part, the church has secured advantages of indisputable value. The Holy See has secured that temporal independence which it has sought in vain for sixty years. As a temporal power it can command greater respect. The material recompense which the church will receive is of no slight importance, especially to a treasury which is at times rather pinched. And, finally, the church has succeeded in putting a Catholic impress on the Italian state—a severe blow to Italian anticlericalism.

As far as immediate appearances are concerned it seems that both parties have won decided advantages at comparatively slight sacrifices. It would seem, too, that there was neither victor nor vanquished in the settlement, that the terms were mutually satisfactory. But whatever the verdict of history may be in this regard, one thing is certain, the accord and its negotiations will find an important place in the annals of both church and state.

4. *Fascist religion.*—The most far-reaching aspect of Fascism's attitude toward religion, though not the most tangible, is the success of the movement in building up its own religious atmosphere and rites. Fascism claims to be not a mere political revolution but a spiritual revolution, initiating a new era in the culture of Italy, if not of the world. As such, it has the rudiments of a new religion. Whether or not these will grow remains to be seen, but certainly there can be no doubt that already this new cult has taken some hold of the Italian heart and imagination.

One of the earliest manifestations of Fascist religiousness was the cult of martyrdom. The victims of the fights with the "subversives" were immediately proclaimed as martyrs: their names were glorified, their memory, sanctified; monuments and tablets were erected in their honor and a large part of the activities of the *fasci* consisted in gathering to celebrate their victories, honor their martyrs, and express their devotion to the cause and eagerness to die in its defense.

Then came the deification of Il Duce—his life is sacred, his word law, and his will the supreme rule of life. The unquestioning obedience demanded of every Fascist is more than military discipline and more than dictatorship; it is the expression of discipleship to a divinely sent leader of the nation. Likewise the black uniform, the black pennant, the Roman salute, the cries of *eia-eia-a-la-lá,* the interminable parades, marches, drills, convocations, celebrations, etc., are not primarily military—they are the rites and ritual of the *fasci.*

And among the Roman elements which have been resurrected to give the appearance of the coming of the new Roman Empire, there are occasional revivals of pagan religious rites. For example, the ceremony (October 27, 1928) of burning the debt certificates, which various individuals and organizations had offered as a "sacrifice on the altar of the country," took place before the tomb of the unknown soldier, on an ancient altar dedicated to Minerva and Lucina, which was taken from the museums for this purpose. This was followed on the next day by the usual "Roman marches" of the Fascist legions celebrating the anniversary of their march on Rome. Meanwhile the Catholic church was proclaiming that day as the feast of Jesus Christ, the king, and was asking for a missionary offering for the "propagation of the faith."

All this may seem quite artificial and even unreal to a foreigner and he may find it impossible to take it all seriously. But even a casual acquaintance with the spirit and inner life of a *fascio* is enough to reveal the emotional appeal and imaginative force which all this exerts on the youth of the nation. Naturally the politicians exploit this fact and carry the whole affair to almost nauseating extremes in their efforts to "discipline" the movement; consequently the bulk of the literature and talk of the party is not to be taken as a sincere expression of actual sentiments, but as sheer propaganda. Nevertheless, there is a considerable and undeniable element of religious conviction and devotion in most Fascists, which transcends the limits of political strife and party tactics.

Catechisms, creeds, spiritual guides, and devotional literature in all its traditional forms are to be found among Fascists in abundance. A few passages selected at random from the typical and fairly moderate *Manuale del Fascista: Regolamento spirituale di disciplina*[4] will illustrate this point:

"I have two sides," says Heroism, "and both are equally beautiful and though their beauty be different they reflect a single Idea: the soul of our Country.

"I have two voices," says Heroism, "and both are equally animating; and though their cries have different sounds, they lead to the same goal; the elevation of the soul of our Country.

"My first side inflamed you with passion and urged you exultingly toward death;

"My second side inflames you with love and leads you exultingly toward the Apostolate.

"My first voice sang to you the song of war; it was the bugle call and the noise of battle;

"My second voice is an austere warning and entrusts to you the task of redemption.

"Once I placed a revolver, hand-grenade and torch in your hand —a tragic necessity demanded by an historic hour—and you struck down your degenerate brother to save your Mother.

[4] By M. Baciocchi de Peón (Florence, 1923).

"Now I cry to you: That hour has passed. The Mother whom you saved from the flood calls you to other proofs of your love.

"I know your youth is rebellious, for it is generous and bubbling over with energy. . . . .

"But in the name of the first, the heroic novitiate of glory, I ask you to devote yourself without stint to the second, the heroic novitiate of the spirit.

"The first was beautiful. Beautiful and sacred is the second.

"It is sacred because it proceeds without external clamor; it pays no attention to applause and does not crown itself with laurel.

"It is sacred because in each of you it works the work of your own redemption in the intimate and insistent travail of your spirits.

"It is sacred because it calls each of you to that priesthood which comes of itself as each of you is made an apostle of social redemption."

Your fallen comrades are coming. They are the dead on the Carso, on the Piave, on the Alps, and on the seas. They are your dead, O young hero.

The dead are coming. They fell in ambushes, in the squares of Italian cities, under the blows of clubs and bombs, singing our country's anthem.

They are your dead, O Fascist.

They are coming. Behold them! They arise, they raise their arms and reach toward you in silence.

They greet you as the new apostle, him who exalts faith and honor, him who summons unto himself with the high voice of passion all those spotless virtues which will make him a moral champion worthy of Rome.

Your dead salute you as the New Italic Soul.

Page after page of such literature is published and, whether it is ever read or not, it at least bears testimony to the emotional upheaval in Fascist authors, and gives some indication of the religious ferment that is current in Italy.

If we turn from the temper of the individual Fascist to the organizations which Fascism has built, their religious character is equally evident. First of all the doctrine and practice of "hierarchy" is common to the Catholic church and the Fascist state, and even to the last detail their tactics and techniques are parallel. Here, for example, is a list of the Catholic organizations of Italy with their Fascist analogues.

The *Azione Cattolica*	The *Instituto Fascista di Cultura*
Federazione Sportiva Cattolica[5] *Esploratori Cattolici*[5]	. *Balilla*
Gioventù Cattolica	*Avanguardia*
Federazione Uomini Cattolici . .	*Fasci*
Unione Femminile Cattolica . . .	*Fasci Femminile*
Gioventù Femminile Cattolica . .	*Giovani Italiane*
Fanciulli Cattolici	*Piccole Italiane*
Universitarie Cattoliche	*Gruppi Universitari Fascista*
Associazione Scrittori Cattolici, etc..	*Federazione Scrittori Fascista,* etc.

This does not imply necessarily that Fascism and Catholicism have been consciously imitating each other's methods, but it does mean that there are in Italy today two and only two great systems of organizations which Italians can join. They are not necessarily incompatible, yet devotion to one is apt to detract from devotion to the other.

In other words, the rivalry between church and state for the souls of Italians is keener now than it ever has been. In Italy the rivalry has been traditional, and since 1870 has been acute. For a few years after the war this situation was changed by the success of the Popularist party. Unaccustomed to the political game in Italy, the church was at first decidedly cool toward Don Sturzo and his party. As soon as its effectiveness was demonstrated, however, the papacy gave it vigorous support, so that for a brief time it looked as though both politics and syndi-

[5] Abolished by the Fascists.

calism would drift into the hands of the church. But this political experiment proved short-lived. Force of circumstances, to which the Fascists contributed, compelled Don Sturzo to ally himself closer and closer with the Socialists. The union of Catholicism and socialism, however, proved too preposterous for the conservative clergy and consequently, when the Fascist Régime brought pressure to bear in 1923, the Pope readily renounced the Popularist party and withdrew from the political game.

Since then the picture is quite clear. Church and state are two distinct institutions and each has a single, highly centralized organization. Each is trying to get its grip on every phase of Italian social and intellectual life. The mere fact that "Fascist," like "Catholic," is now an adjective which can be applied to anything whatsoever is significant.

The most open and decisive conflict which has occurred in this field is the conflict between the Catholic boys' organizations (the Catholic Scouts and Catholic Athletic Association) and the Fascist Balilla. The way in which these organizations conflict is too obvious to need exposition. The Fascists at first abolished these Catholic organizations only in small places of less than 20,000 inhabitants, but in 1927 they abolished all of them, and Balilla now has a complete monopoly of the field of boys' clubs. The church then founded the Fanciulli Cattolici, with the understanding that this new organization would confine itself to strictly religious activities. Hence the Fanciulli Cattolici meet to learn the catechism; they have catechism contests, make pilgrimmages to Rome, etc. But one can readily imagine how much more attractive Balilla is.

The other Catholic organizations, especially the Azione Cattolica, are also compelled to be strictly religious, or at most philanthropic institutions. They may not engage in politics or any other form of activity covered by the Fascist organizations.

The creation of the corporate state raised this same issue in a slightly different form. Only legally recognized syndicates, co-operatives, and professional associations are allowed according to the corporate law and these must, of course, be Fascist. The Catholic associations immediately feared that this was aimed at them and made inquiry. The minister of corporations replied that strictly religious associations would not come under the laws of the corporate state. The Catholic co-operatives were permitted to join the Fascist Association of Co-operatives. All other Catholic societies are simply ignored.

All these events tend in one direction: the bipolarization of Italian society and culture in two great institutions, each competing for the first place in the minds and affections of the people. The organizations of the church are being limited wherever possible to strictly religious activities except in so far as the state legally intrusts other functions (for example, education) to the church, and all this is done at the dictation of the state. The church has protested and officially "grieved," but it has complied with the government's orders. Meanwhile the state is building up a set of organizations which tend to place the cult of the nation in the foreground of the daily thought and imagination of the people.

This thoroughgoing cult of the nation, pursued by the great variety of techniques which we discuss in this volume, and aimed, as it is, primarily at the next generation, will inevitably have a telling effect on the prestige of the church. This insertion of the state into the fundamental emotions, manners, ideas, and celebrations of the people is all the more effective because it does not attack the church. It is thoroughly Catholic! But the government knows, and so does the church, that if this religion of the nation continues to make its appeal as it is now doing, it will put the church and the whole traditional content of Christianity into the background.

An attempt to predict the outcome of the rivalry between these two cults would be out of place here. Suffice it to point out that beneath the surface of cordiality which exists between church and state, a profound conflict is emerging, involving not only the political fortunes of the Fascist Régime, but also the whole form and content of Italian civilization.

PART II
TECHNIQUES OF CIVIC TRAINING

CHAPTER V

FASCIST EDUCATION

1. *Public education in Italy.*—The public school is by far the most efficacious means of winning the allegiance of a nation's youth to national ideals. The educational experiments of the French revolutionists demonstrated to the nations the use of the elementary school for civic training. To a certain extent the nationalist mission of the school is not an innovation in Italy. The Casati Law, of November 13, 1859, provided for free public instruction, and the Coppino Law, of July 15, 1877, made attendance compulsory until the age of twelve. Despite this legislation Italy's educational system was not so efficient as it should have been. Many of the towns required to build schools took no action. Parents thought their children economically more valuable at work in the fields or factories than in the classroom. Moreover tradition had assigned whatever education was necessary to the church and naturally the church was very loath to turn over this most important function to the state. Those public schools which did exist were not particularly efficient. An attempt was made to improve them by the Credaro Law (1911), which provided for strict state control and state aid, but legislation proved futile wherever local authorities had no faith in national laws.

This being the situation, illiteracy naturally remained an important problem. The percentage of literate people in Italy was 31 in 1872, 52 in 1901, 62 in 1911, and 73 in 1921. Conditions in the South have been especially bad. For instance, in Sicily only 51 per cent of the population can read; in Calabria the percentage is 47; in Basilicata it is 48; in Sardinia, 51. Greater progress has been made in the North. In Piedmont 93 per cent of the population can read; in Liguria 91 per cent; in Lombardy 91; and in South Tyrol (formerly Austrian territory) 98 per cent.[1]

Educational conditions vary regionally exactly with the amount of illiteracy. For instance, in Sicily of the 110,117 children who should have gone to school in 1924–25, only 83,136 were enrolled; only 71,826 actually attended classes, and only 4,087 were promoted. On the other hand, the respective figures for Piedmont were 336,030; 313,256; 276,991, and 246,917. For the entire kingdom: 4,818,436; 3,644,606; 3,205,420, and 2,233,-933.[2]

2. *The Fascist theory of civic education.*—The Fascists determined to better conditions, realizing that the schools were necessary for their propaganda and that an illiterate population could only with great difficulty be made to comprehend the Fascist Revolution and the aims of the Régime. Under the direction of Giovanni Gentile, a complete reform was undertaken in order to establish schools for building character—national and religious character.[3] This emphasis meant that national tradition was to become the very heart of the curriculum and that, as a result, the national state itself would become a living force in Italian life. Consequently this reform has been called the most Fascist of all the acts of the Régime.[4] It forces all children to attend school until the age of four-

[1] *Annuario Statistico Italiano* (Rome, 1927); *Istituto Centrale di Statistica* (1927), pp. 67–68.

[2] See also the complete table, *op. cit.*, p. 69.

[3] Giovanni Gentile, *Che cosa è il Fascismo* (Florence: Vallechi, 1925), pp. 163–66.

[4] See Gentile, *Il Fascismo al Governo della Scuola*, pp. 250–53.

teen; it introduces new pedagogic methods and a new curriculum, and it floods the educational system from kindergarten to university with Fascist doctrine.[5]

Two days after the formation of the Mussolini cabinet, the new minister of public instruction, Gentile, sent the following greeting to Italian educational authorities:

I come to the Ministry of Public Instruction with my former faith in the destinies of our civilization and in the spirit of our schools renewed. The greater the trial, the greater has always been the ability of the Italians to surpass themselves, and the more ready the school to raise an admonishing voice and to serve as an example. I call to my support all Italian teachers, urging them to work with new vigor for the future of our Country.[6]

The new minister, imbued with Hegelianism and ardent nationalism, expected to use the schools for teaching nationalism.

We affirm our belief that the State is not a system of hindrances and external juridical controls from which men flee, but an ethical being which, like the conscience of the individual, manifests its personality and achieves its historical growth in human society. Thus it is conscious not of being hedged in by special limits, but of being open, ready, and capable of expanding as a collective and yet individual will. The nation is that will, conscious of itself and of its own historical past, which, as we formulate it in our minds, defines and delineates our nationality, generating an end to be attained, a mission to be realized. For that will, in case of need, our lives are sacrificed, for our lives are genuine, worthy, and endowed with incontestable value only as they are spent in the accomplishment of that mission.

The State's active and dynamic consciousness is a system of thought, of ideas, of interests to be satisfied and of morality to be realized. Hence the State is, as it ought to be, a teacher; it maintains and develops schools to promote this morality. In the school the State comes to a consciousness of its real being.

[5] *Ibid.*, pp. 207–37, 248; G. Lombardo-Radice, *Vita Nuova della Scuola del Popolo* (Palermo: Sandron, 1925), pp. xxxv–lxvi.

[6] Circular of November 2, 1922. Published in Gentile, *Il Fascismo al Governo della Scuola* (Palermo: Sandron, 1924), p. 9.

The chief implications of this idealistic philosophy for the theory of education may be briefly summarized as follows:

(1) The real mind of the child reveals itself in action, not in the abstract forms of verbal "knowledge": Hence the school must train the behavior of the child and teach it to realize the implications or meaning of its acts. Knowledge is acquired by functioning in the behavior-patterns of the child and hence the "abstractions" of book learning must give place in the curriculum to the "concrete" forms of active thought, which are found only in "self-mastery through conquest of opposition," that is, of ignorance, perplexities, problems, or anything "external." All "bodies of knowledge," all sciences and their laws are abstractions from action, and by the process of education must be transformed into action.

(2) It follows that the center of educational subject matter and method is the individual character and not certain traditional "subjects" of information: From the elementary schools up to the universities, the aim is to develop unified and disciplined personalities. This is to be accomplished not only by vocational education but also by the student's active participation in all the institutions and traditions of his people.

(3) Moral personality is achieved by the identification of the individual with the culture of his nation: In a sense, culture is universal; but universal culture "develops its own inner multiplicity" by means of national cultures, which have their several limitations and hence their opportunities of growth and spiritual conquest. Each moral individual must transcend himself, not merely by identifying himself with the nation's traditions or culture (as the professional nationalists teach) but also by engaging in the process of spiritual growth or conquest

whereby the boundaries of his own, and hence of his nation's, experience and culture are widened and the "external world" is transcended by the creative act of will and thought.

(4) The political implication is that moral freedom is attained by an inner sharing in the cultural and traditional life of the people, not by a formal and mechanical participation in democratic institutions: Liberty is not an a priori right, but a moral obligation, to be won only by voluntarily serving the national will. This national will can find unified expression only if the state is able to synthesize the various institutions of the national life. The chief instrument for bringing about such a unity is a unified system of national education.

(5) The religious implications are that the individual can live in the universal spirit only through the national spirit, and that the people is more "catholic" than its church: Therefore the church must be embodied in the state, and religion must be taught in the national schools by secular teachers. Elementary religious education consists in teaching familiarity with, and active participation in, the traditional religion of the people, with all its myths and superstitions. Then gradually the critical element is introduced, and traditional religion becomes transformed into a self-conscious, national idealism—not by means of abstract criticism and indoctrination, but through the intimate and personal growth of the individual mind.[7]

3. *The organization of the school system.*—The practical application of this theory of national education is intrusted to the minister of instruction who is aided in general educational policy by a Superior Council of Public Instruction, composed of twenty-one members chosen by the minister himself;[8] in matters of higher education by

---

[7] Cf. chap. iv.   [8] This Council was formerly elective.

a section of this Council, and in elementary and secondary school affairs by two commissions.[9] That the minister's orders may be carried out, there are three central inspectors, men in whom he has complete confidence.[10]

For purposes of local school administration Italy is divided into nineteen districts, each one under a *Provveditore,* a sort of state superintendent of schools, who is appointed by the minister.[11] He is aided in the administration of elementary school affairs by a Scholastic Council and a Disciplinary Council (the members of both are appointed by ministerial decree), the duties of the former being to give advice on important school questions and of the latter to attend to the discipline of teachers.[12] Italy is divided into 250 school districts under scholastic inspectors (*Ispettori Scolastici*), or subsuperintendents, and these districts are in turn divided into about 2,000 smaller regions under directors of pedagogy. Both the inspectors and the directors are chosen by competitive examinations.[13] Certain towns—the capitals of the provinces and districts (*circondaria*)—have educational autonomy and hence do not come within the foregoing organization. Their schools are directed by city superintendents but are under the supervision of the state, for the central inspectors oversee the entire educational system.[14]

[9] Laws and decrees of February 17, 1908; February 2, 1913; December 31, 1923, Art. 1, and February 4, 1926.

[10] Law of December 31, 1923, Art. 2, 3, and 4.

[11] Decree of November 3, 1923, Art. 1. A handy collection of the laws which embodied the Gentile reforms is found in Giuseppe Lombardo-Radice, *Vita Nuova della Scuola del Popolo* (Palermo: Sandron, 1925).

[12] Decree of November 3, 1923, Art. 2–6. For the duties of these bodies see the Ministerial Decree of June 5, 1924, Art. 1. For administrative purposes the superintendent has a Scholastic Office Decree of November 5, 1923, Art. 8.

[13] Decree of November 3, 1923, Art. 9–13.

[14] Decree of November 3, 1923, Arts. 14–17.

Secondary education is also under the general direction of the *Provveditori,* who are advised by Councils for Secondary Schools, by the local principals (*Preside*), and by the inspectors (*Ispettori delle Scuole Medie*).[15] Universities are under the direction of rectors appointed by ministerial decree.

Education in the elementary schools is divided into three grades: the *Grado Preparatorio,* three years of kindergarten for children between the ages of three and five; the *Grado Inferiore,* three years; and the *Grado Superiore,* two years.[16] A school year is normally ten months, or at least 180 days.[17]

After completing the higher grade, pupils attend the secondary schools for at least three years, as school attendance is compulsory until the age of fourteen.[18] To fulfil this requirement pupils may either take the *corsi integrativi,* which supplement the education of the higher grade, or enter a complementary school—a sort of trade and junior high school. If they intend to continue their secondary education they enter *ginnasi* (junior high schools), where they study for five years and then enter either classical or scientific high schools *(licei),* where they take a three-year course preparatory to the universities. Those pupils who desire to train themselves for public employment, for industrial engineering, agriculture, commerce, etc., proceed after the *Grado Superiore* of the elementary schools to technical institutions, where they may study for either four or eight years. Those who wish to train themselves for the teaching profession enter normal schools (*Istituti Magistrali*) for a preparatory

[15] Law of January 22, 1925, Art. 7, and Decree of April 30, 1924, Arts. 1, 8, and 23.

[16] Decree of October 1, 1923, Art. 1.

[17] Decree of October 1, 1923, Art. 14.

[18] Decree of December 31, 1923.

course of four years and then an advanced course of three years. Girls who desire a secondary education may take either the regular courses in *ginnasi* and *licei,* or a three years' cultural course in girls' finishing schools *(licei femminili).* Entrance to these institutions presupposes a four years' preparatory course, which is usually obtained in the preparatory course of the normal schools. The institution of these girls' finishings schools is an innovation.[19] After the secondary schools the student may continue his education in a university, where the length of the course varies according to the studies pursued.

The cost of the public educational system is shared between the state and the cities, the former subsidizing secondary and higher institutions, and the latter financing for the most part elementary schools. In 1925 the state spent 1,364,091,000 lire, and the cities, 467,611,000 lire, a total of 1,831,702,000 lire.[20] This sum seems astounding until it is compared with the expenditure for national defense in the same year, which was 4,434,310,-000 lire. It must also be remembered that in addition to the public school system there are private institutions— especially Catholic—which are of no mean importance in Italy, although their budgets are not great, since their teachers are almost all celibates and are paid very little.

4. *The curriculum.*—Although it is necessary to comprehend the structure of the Italian educational system in order to understand the part played by the schools in civic training, it is of more vital importance to know what the children are taught. On the whole, with the hope that the initiative of the teachers would develop the best in their pupils, administrative authorities and teachers in the various regions are given a great deal of liberty to

[19] Decree of May 6, 1923.

[20] *Annuario Statistico* (1927), pp. 309 and 333.

adapt their programs to particular local needs.[21] The program given in Table III was established, however, as a general guide for elementary education.[22]

It will be noticed from this standard outline that considerable emphasis is placed on language in the first years

TABLE III

ELEMENTARY SCHOOLS

SUBJECTS	YEARS						
	Preparatory	I	II	III	IV	V	Supplementary*
	Hours per Week						
Religion	1	1½	1½	2	2	2	2
Singing, drawing, and recitation	4	2½	2½	4	5	5	3
Reading and writing		7	6	5	5	4	3
Orthography			2	2			
Arithmetic		4	4	4	3	3	2
Various recreative intellectual occupations	6	4	4	4	1	1	1
Gardening, manual training, gymnastics, hygiene, and domestic training	24	6	5	4	4	4	
Natural and physical science					2	2	3
History and geography					3	3	2
Civics and economics						1	1
Professional work							8
Total	35 Thursday included	25	25	25	25	25	25

* *Corsi integrativi.*

so that, if for any reason the child does not continue his studies, he will be able to read and write. Also instruction

[21] Ministerial Order of November 11, 1923, printed with other orders pertaining to the same subject in *Nuovi Programmi per le Scuole Elementari* (Naples: E. Pietrocola, 1925). The programs for the other schools are published by the same house. Some results of this system have been judged by G. Lombardo-Radice, *Athena Fanciula* (Florence: Bemporad, 1928), and by Riccardo Dalpiaz, *Esperienze Didattiche di un Ispettore Trentino* (Rome: Associazione per il Mezzogiorno, 1928).

[22] Ministerial Order of November 11, 1923.

in the Catholic religion has been reintroduced into the schools.[23] The church is authorized to supervise both teachers and texts for this instruction. Lessons in religion are given by the regular teachers unless they are declared incompetent. It has been charged that this reform was a political move, for religion is taught only in the elementary schools, and is replaced in the secondary institutions by philosophy. The Catholics maintain that what is good for one is good for all. Gentile has answered personal attacks on the "opportunism" of the reform by stating that this was his program prior to Fascism.[24] Considerable time is left for the initiative of the teacher in the various recreative intellectual occupations. History is not taught until the third year, and only one hour is devoted to civics in the fifth year.

It would seem from a study of the schedule that no special attempt is made to emphasize nationalism, but such is not the case. In the second year, during the time allowed for various recreational intellectual occupations, the teacher must "relate episodes of civil, religious, and military valor . . . . ," explaining the faith necessary for making sacrifices for the country.[25] In the third year the teacher must read or relate stories to the children to develop their historical and national consciousness, relying for his themes on the lives of great men (Garibaldi and Battisti among others) ; and in the fourth and fifth years he must give a series of readings to illustrate the regional contributions to the life of the nation, especially during the period of Italian unification.[26] During the courses of gymnastics the life of a soldier must be portrayed as an example of strength, discipline, and courage.

[23] Decree of October 1, 1923, Art. 3.

[24] Gentile, *Il Fascismo al Governo della Scuola*, pp. 212–14.

[25] Ministerial Order of November 11, 1923.   [26] *Ibid.*

During the geography lessons especial attention must be given to a study of the city, historical places in the region, the physical and political nature of Italy, and of foreign countries, especially those to which Italian emigrants have gone. The study of history begins in the third year with Italian history from 1848 to 1918, the general course being supplemented by the readings of the most significant proclamations, letters, and memoirs of national martyrs, and the orders of the *condottieri*. In the fourth year ancient history is prescribed with emphasis on ancient Rome. In the fifth year the pupils study Italian history during the period of foreign domination (with emphasis on the history of the province), the works of Italian artists (especially local ones), events of Italian history during the nineteenth century, the Italian army and navy, the great heroes and brilliant episodes of the Great War, the great public works undertaken after the unification of Italy, and a comparison of the national wealth with that of other countries. After the fifth year (in the *corsi integrativi*) the pupils must read at least one popular but well-known history, study the Italian colonies, and get some "notions" of foreign countries. Even in religious instruction especial attention must be paid to *Italian* saints.[27] In addition to all this there are the reading lessons, which from the programs might not seem to be nationalistic but which are in reality extremely patriotic.

5. *Textbooks and patriotic materials.*—As a further guaranty that the instruction shall be of the kind desired, a decree was issued prohibiting the use of textbooks which had not been approved by the state.[28] A special Commission was appointed to censor all the texts published prior

[27] *Ibid.*

[28] Decree of March 11, 1923. Eventually the *Provveditori* will supervise the approval of these books (Art. 5).

to the reform. This Commission examined 1,710 readers, definitely approved 32 of them as texts, 173 provisionally for one year, and 32 for reference. They examined 317 histories, definitely approving 125, provisionally accepting 73, and declaring 18 suitable for school libraries, and refusing 101. Of the 114 books for religious instruction, 11 were approved, 35 accepted for one year, 39 declared suitable for libraries, and 29 definitely refused.[29] Despite this strict censorship of school texts the Fascist leaders are not satisfied and they are studying a project whereby the state will have texts written according to its dictates and furnish them to the schools.[30]

The report of the Textbook Commission concerning readers included many general recommendations, among others that these books should not "present an abstract Country, but should instill a love for Italy. . . . ."[31] The way in which patriotism is preached by these readers may be gathered from a study of several of the most important ones.[32]

(1) Renato Franceschini, *Sillabario Moderno e Piccole Letture.* Florence: Bemporad, 1928.

This little first-year reader is in its thirty-fourth edition and its 572d thousand. It has been definitely approved by the state. It is very elementary, beginning with the alphabet and simple words. It

[29] Report of the Commission in Giuseppi Lombardo-Radice, *Scuole, Maestri, e Libri* (Palermo: Sandron, 1926), p. 310, Dario Lupi, *La Riforma Gentile e la Nuova Anima della Scuola* (Rome: Mondadori, 1924), pp. 58–59.

[30] Declaration by Minister Fedele and Mussolini to the Chamber in *Atti Parlamentari, Camera dei Deputati* (1926), pp. 5,783.

[31] See the report published in G. Lombardo-Radice, *Scuole, Maestri, e Libri*, p. 309.

[32] In order that he might criticize only those books which are most widely used, the author asked Signore Giuseppe Lombardo-Radice, who is the director of elementary schools in Rome and the man responsible for most of the Gentile reform laws concerning primary education, to make a list of the readers, histories, and civics texts which have the greatest sales. A complete list of Italian schoolbooks is to be found in a catalogue, *Libri Scolastici* (Milan: Associazione Editoriale Libreria Italiana, 1927).

has three short patriotic exhortations, the most nationalistic of which is: "Dear and sweet is the name of our Country. We children want to be good patriots, too."[33]

(2) Ciro Trabalza, Vincenzina Battistelli, and Luisa Steiner, *Militi del Lavoro*. Florence: Bemporad, 1928.

This second year reader is the second volume of a series for all grades. It is in its eleventh edition and has received the definite approval of the Ministry of Public Instruction. Five of its 158 pages are devoted to patriotism. On pages 55–56 one may read:

"Every good Italian loves Italy, this land so great and beautiful. And every little Italian should study in order to be an honor to his country, in order to be able to read some day the works of her poets, and in order to know her history and her beauty. And then, children, when you know how great your country has been through the centuries, what marvellous things Italians have always been able to do, then you will love her still more and say with an air of pride, 'I am an Italian.'"

(3) G. Marchi and V. Battistelli, *Biancospino*. Florence: Bemporad, 1925.

This reader for the third year is one of a series for the elementary schools. It has been definitely approved by the state. Ten of its 184 pages are devoted to a patriotic lesson about Garibaldi. The story relates how an old Garibaldian had those who went to fight in the World War kiss a handkerchief stained by the blood of Garibaldi. The old man exhorted the mother and friends to write the soldiers that whoever "has kissed the blood of Garibaldi cannot be a coward. Dying one must either kiss the Italian flag or bite the enemy."[34] In the same lesson there is a picture of poppies and potatoes, the former representing red-shirted Garibaldians and the latter Austrians. Above it is written: "Bing! Bang! And the Austrians are dead."

(4) Virgilio Brocchi and Andrea Gustarelli, *Allegretto e Sevenella*. Milan: Mondadori, 1925.

This reader for the fourth year is one of a series for elementary schools. It has been definitely approved by the state. About 25 of its 221 pages are devoted to patriotic subjects. On page 90 one reads:

"There have been great men everywhere, in France, in England, in Germany, all over Europe as well as in America and Asia. But fortune has particularly smiled on Italy, for she seems to have inher-

[33] P. 55.   [34] Pp. 52–53.

ited from Ancient Rome the mission of teaching beauty, law, and science to other peoples.

"The first among the great poets of modern times was, as you know, Dante, an Italian. The most wonderful artists who have ever lived . . . . were Italians—Leonardo da Vinci, Raphael, and Michelangelo. The very beautiful musicians from Palestrina to Claudio Monteverde, who have been the masters of our great composers and of foreigners in the divine art of music, were Italians."

On pages 39–40 there is this story:

" 'Do you know who Pasquale Sottocorno was?' asked the teacher.

" 'No,' confessed Cippelletti.

" 'He was a shoemaker from Milan. He was lame on account of a bad hip. In 1848 the Revolution broke out. Milan flew unarmed at the oppressors. The Artillery bombarded the barricades. The Captain of the citizens said, "Men, you must attack the palace of the Military Engineers and knock down the door. . . . ." But no one dared to move, for between the barricade and the Palace there was a straight road swept with grape-shot. Then Pasquale Sottocorno, limping with his crutch, crossed the street under the whistling of the bullets, and came to the door of the Palace. He fired it with an armful of oakum dipped in kerosene and forced two hundred Austrians to surrender.

" 'What courage!' exclaimed Cippelletti.

" 'What a noble mind,' added the teacher. Then she said, 'Which seems greater, nobler, and more honest—this shoemaker or the King of Naples, Duke of Modena? Would you prefer to have been Pasquale Sottocorno or Francis IV?'

" 'Oh, a thousand times more Pasquale Sottocorno,' exclaimed the boy."

(5) Michele Mastropaolo, *La Dolce Campania*. Milan: Vallardi, 1926.

In the new educational programs especial emphasis is placed on regional history and culture. In the third, fourth, and fifth years the children must have a regional reader and almanac. The present book is one of a series of such a nature, being written for the pupils of Campania Province (Naples and environs). It has received ministerial approval. On the whole it has very little Italian nationalism although there is one passage (p. 12) concerning the contribution of the region to the Italian victory in the World War. It is full, however, of regionalism, exhorting the beauties of Naples, Capri, Avellino, and other places, praising the great men who have come from this district, describing in a picturesque way the various Neapolitan holidays. For example, on page 7, there is this statement:

"The Campania is one of the most beautiful regions in Italy. It comprises five departments: Naples, Caserta, Salerno, Avellino, and Benevento. . . . . The Campania is making steady progress in industry, trade, culture, and art. Let us help her increase her wealth, prestige, and civilization by our work and education. Let us make her one of the best regions of Italy.

"It is our vow.

"It shall be our duty!"

(6) Luigi Ambrosini, *Nuove Pagine di Vita*. Turin: Paravia.

This book is a reader for the *corsi integrativi*, complementary schools, and the first years of the secondary schools. It has no date nor statement as to state approval. Out of 316 pages 7 are devoted to pure nationalism, 20 to the customs of the Romans, many to regionalism, and a great many to great Italians—Giotto, Dante, Leonardo da Vinci, Leopardi, Columbus, Mazoni, Mazzini, and others. A quotation from Mazzini relates how he became conscious of the necessity of fighting for Italy's liberty. In 1821 he and his parents were walking in Genoa when a man accosted them and asked alms "for those ostracized from Italy." "That day was the first time that there was presented to my mind, not the idea of Country and liberty, but the idea that one should fight for the liberty of the Country."[35]

The Textbook Commission's report on history books was drawn up by a man of sound judgment and considerable historical training, Giuseppe Prezzolini. It criticized the habitual use of traditional figures whose chief contributions to history have been the utterance of some "historical" phrases or the achievement of some isolated acts, and the exclusion of more obscure men who have played great rôles in history. For instance, the person of Christ is usually referred to in a sentimental way without reference to the other founders of Christian institutions. In the history of the *risorgimento* many pages are devot-

[35] P. 286.

ed to Mazzini and very few to Manzoni or Leopardi. The
social and economic questions of this period are usually
entirely omitted. "The most mediocre authors in writing
for children enjoy narrating in detail stories of brutal-
ities, cruelties, atrocities, and passion. Such stories as
that of the Anconian mother who offered her breast to a
soldier to nourish him, and that of Carlo Zima who was
tarred and burned by the Austrians, are immoral and exhibit bad taste. . . . ." In general the Commission maintained that all the period of contemporary history should
be rewritten on account of the disproportionate emphasis
given during the post-war period to colonial wars, earth-
quakes, and explosions, as though they were great national events. The Commission desired that the rural classes
(usually neglected) as well as labor, industry, commerce,
and all the forces of Italy, be given the place they de-
serve, and that men and events be pictured in just pro-
portions.[36] Unfortunately Italian history textbooks have
not been reformed according to the Commission's report,
as will be seen from the following books:

(1) Franco Ciarlantini, *Storia Italiana.* Milan: Mondadori,
1925.

This text is for first-year history classes, that is, for the pupil's
third year. It is one of a series prepared for all classes. It has the
approval of the state. The interpretation of Italian history in this
book is very nationalistic. It covers the nineteenth and twentieth
centuries, but almost all the space is devoted to the *risorgimento* and
the World War. The book is filled with minor but dramatic anecdotes
(pp. 17, 24, 48, 49, 53, 54, 58, etc.). Especial emphasis is placed on
the heroes of the *risorgimento* (S. Pellico, Mazzini, Garibaldi, and
Cavour) and of the World War (Generals Cadorna and Diaz, Cesare
Battisti and Nazario Sauro, Austrian subjects who deserted to serve
for Italy but were taken prisoners and killed). The book begins with
these words:

[36] Report of the Commission in Lombardo-Radice, *Scuole, Maestri, e Libri,* pp. 314–17.

"Italy, our Country, has not always been a united and free nation. Our grandfathers remember the sad times when foreigners were masters in our homes, when the Country was divided into many little states and the citizens were subjected to all sorts of outrages and did not have the right to protest.

"Those were sad times, children!"

The book ends with this passage:

"In Eternal Rome, on the historical hills of Campidoglio, rises the monument of Italian Independence in the center of which is erected the statue of the Gentleman King.

"At the foot of the statue there is an altar called the Altar of the Fatherland. There an urn of pure marble contains the bones of one of the thousands and thousands of soldiers who fell without leaving a trace of their names.

"This is the Tomb of the Unknown Soldier who represents all the dead of our War and to whose memory has been awarded the Golden Medal with this inscription:

"'This worthy son of a valiant race and of a rich civilization, held without flinching those trenches most bitterly contested, displayed courage in the most cruel battles, and fell fighting for no other end than that his Country might be victorious and great.'"

(2) Angelo Magni, *Italia! Italia!* Milan: Mondadori.

This book is a history text for the sixth year (the *corsi integrativi*). It is in its sixth edition and the 60th thousand. It has been approved by the state. It bears no date.

The period covered by this text is 1800 to the present time, but the emphasis is placed on the *risorgimento* and the World War. It is patriotic throughout. On page 29 one reads concerning the *risorgimento*:

"The little revolts awakened revolutionary ideas in people's minds. The horrors and cruelties of the police and governments aroused them—even the callous and timid—to an ardent desire for revenge. Arms are all right, but one must first arouse the desire to use them. One must first awaken a sentiment in the hearts of the people and stir up their spirits so that every citizen will feel ashamed to see his Country a slave and will become a soldier to redeem her at the cost of his life."

The book is filled with anecdotes of heroes and battles. S. Pellico, Mazzini, Cavour, Garibaldi, and Victor Emmanuel II are all treated at length. In the story of the World War the book explains that Italy entered the conflict to get Trent, Trieste, and other territories, and to fight for the right of humanity.[37]

(3) Nuccio e Tancredi, *Giovinezza Eroica*. Palermo: *Industrie Riunite Editoriali Siciliane,* 1926.

This text is an "historical reader for patriotic education," for the *corsi integrativi,* and complementary schools. It has the approval of the state. It treats the *risorgimento* and the World War and Fascism. Almost every page is patriotic. The book itself says:

"Reading these pages you will learn to love still more the blessed land where you were born, every clod of whose soil has been stained with the blood of a hundred martyrs. You will learn to respect her laws. Through her organizations and institutions you will learn to defend her against all invasions and against decadence. You will learn to live and die for her with her beloved name on your lips."[38]

About fifty pages are devoted to Fascism, explaining that the Fascist Revolution saved the country from Bolshevism. The Russian situation is described as deplorable, the comparison between the two states being decidedly in favor of Italy.[39]

As we have already seen, instruction in civics and elementary economics begins in the fifth year and is continued in the *corsi integrativi* and complementary schools, one hour a week being devoted to these subjects. Previous to the fifth year teachers may use the hours for reading or intellectual recreation for teaching the elements of civics. In this way the children are taught the Fascist conception of the state and Fascist philosophy. An idea of the nature of this instruction may be had from the textbooks used.

(1) Pietro Gorgolini, *Il Fascismo Spiegato al Popolo*. Turin: Paravia, 1926.

This book is a popular and simple treatise on Fascism. It is not properly a textbook but has had a wide influence and is used in the schools. It gives a short description of Italy prior to Fascism, then the march on Rome, Fascist philosophy, and Fascist reforms. Mussolini is highly praised. On pages 90–91 one reads:

[37] Pp. 141–42.   [38] P. 8.   [39] Pp. 150–94.

"Now we have the Man who was needed and whom we wanted. He finds himself face to face with great problems. His task is very hard and he is charged with tremendous responsibilities: to reconstruct the patrimony of the Nation; to restore the provinces; to free laws from demagogy; to destroy parasitic forces and parasites; to affirm the rights and dignity of the Nation abroad.

"This man with a Garibaldian spirit and with mailed fist will overcome these difficulties; of this we are sure. But all the citizens of every class must follow him and aid him with faith and abnegation. . . . ."

(2) Valerio Campogrando, *L'Ordinamento dello Stato Italiano Fascista*. Turin: Lattes, 1928.

This book is for the complementary schools. It is in its fourth edition. It is an excellent brief treatise of Fascist reforms. It lauds the régime and its chief. On page 6 is this passage:

"As there is only one official religion of the State, the Catholic, so today there must be only one political faith, Fascism, which is synonymous with the Italian Nation. As the Catholic must have a blind belief in the Catholic faith and obey the Catholic Church blindly, so the perfect Fascist must believe absolutely in the principles of Fascism and obey the hierarchical heads to whom he owes allegiance without reserve.

"Religious dogmas are not discussed because they are truths revealed by God. Fascist principles are not discussed because they come from the mind of a Genius: Benito Mussolini. . . . ."

(3) Umberto Vecchiotti, *Nozione di Economia e Diritto*. Turin: Paravia, 1928.

This book is an elementary civics and economics text. It has been approved by the state. It explains Fascism, but is not nationalistic.

In addition to the influence of the patriotic material in textbooks, Italian school children are surrounded with nationalist symbols. The lictor's rods, emblem of imperial Rome and Fascism, must be worked into every new educational building. In the classrooms of both elementary and secondary schools there must be a crucifix, a picture of the king, and a picture of Mussolini.[40] Many of the classrooms have the announcement of victory drawn

[40] Umberto Renda, *"Scuola e Fascismo"* in *Civiltà Fascista*, p. 477.

up by General Diaz.[41] The Fascists desire that every
day's work begin with a prayer and a national hymn, that
the schools have pictures of the heroes of the *risorgimento,*
of the Great War, and of the masters of Italian culture,
that every school have its flag, and that on the eve of
every vacation a patriotic speech be made and that the
children respond with the Roman salute.[42]

6. *Selection of teachers.*—Despite this patriotic environment and patriotic textbooks, the education of the
children would not necessarily be nationalistic if the
teachers were not nationalists. The Fascists have realized
this, and have taken especial pains to see that the instruc-
ors have the desired political views. A law has been made
whereby teachers may be discharged if they have political
views contrary to those of the government.[43] Although
only four elementary school-teachers have been discharged on political grounds there is always the danger
that they may be, which tends to make them toe the mark.[44]
In order to be appointed to a teaching position one must
pass competitive examinations, preference being given
first to those who were decorated in the war, secondly to
those who have passed other competitive examinations,
thirdly to those who have published their works, and
fourthly "to those who have other qualifications."[45] In
1923 the first examinations for elementary teachers held

[41] See *Nuovi Programmi per le Scole Elementari* (Naples: Pietrocola,
1925), which contains Ordinances of November 11, 1923, and January 21, 1924,
and Decree of December 16, 1923, pp. 36, 52 ff.

[42] Umberto Renda, *op. cit.,* p. 489.

[43] Decree of January 25, 1923, Law of December 24, 1925, Circular of the
Head of the Government, July 22, 1926, and Decree of January 13, 1927,
Art. 5.

[44] This information was given the author by a member of a Commission
appointed to examine the teachers.

[45] Ministerial Decree of June 5, 1924. Art. 38; Lombardo-Radice, *Scuole,
Maestri, e Libri,* p. 185.

by the Régime attracted great numbers—in Piedmont 2,-322, 165 of whom were accepted; in Lombardy 3,108, of whom 677 were approved; in Venetia 1,764, of whom 573 were accepted[46]—in spite of the fact that Italian teachers are paid very little, from 5,600 to 9,500 lire a year plus bonuses which vary from 300 to 1,300 lire.[47] The examinations placed special emphasis on the *risorgimento* and warned the applicants that "no Italian educator could be accepted if he had not read such books as: *Da Quarto al Vatturno* or *La Storia dei Mille* as related for youths by Abba; *Ricordanze* by Settembrini; *Villa Gloria* by Pascarella; *I Matiri di Belfiore* by Luzio, and so on, the most patriotic works of Italian historical literature.

An attempt is made to bring the teachers into the National Fascist Association of Primary School-Teachers, which has a membership at the present time of 80,000. It aims, "first, to encourage the general cultural education of the teachers; and secondly, to expound the new concept of life, of history, and of the Nation which Fascism has affirmed to be the keystone of its action and of its future."[48] Members are influenced by the Association's journal, *La Scuola Fascista,* by frequent congresses, and by the calls of a traveling secretary. It is affiliated with the Fascist party, being attached to the secretariat as all other associations of state employees.

Finally there are the educational reviews—*Educazione Fascista, Annali dell' Istruzione Elementare,* and *Educazione Nazionale*—which bring the nationalist ideas of the educational leaders to the rank and file of the teachers. In these ways, then, Fascism attempts to control the nationalist sentiments of the teachers.

[46] See Lombardo-Radice, *op. cit.,* pp. 212 ff.

[47] Dario Lupi, *La Riforma Gentile,* pp. 44–45.

[48] Art. 4 of Statutes.

7. *Secondary schools.*—In comparison with the elementary schools the secondary schools (for students above fourteen years of age) have played a small part in Italian civic training, but Fascism's most serious efforts at reform have been made precisely in this field. There are, of course, fewer secondary than elementary schools, but their variety is imposing, and much of this variety is the work of Fascism.

A definite attempt has been made to reduce the number of students in secondary schools by making entrance more difficult so that these numbers may in time be even smaller.[49]

In the secondary schools the teaching is more critical and less romantic, although there is still some emotional patriotism as may be gathered from the following textbooks:[50]

(1) Adolfo Amadeo, *L'Età Moderna e Contemporaneo.* Rome: Messina, 1925.

This is the third volume of a series for history in secondary schools and normal schools. The other two volumes were: Ettore Ciccotti, *Il Medio Evo, 476–1313;* and Francesco Cognasso, *Il Rinascimento, 1313–1748.* The series is one of the most widely used in Italian secondary schools.

On the whole this book is very impartial. It treats not only Italian history but also European history in general. It is largely political in its nature but not excessively nationalist. It treats Mazzini, Cavour, and Garibaldi, but in a fairly impartial way and omits the patriotic anecdotes. It mentions the names of war heroes but does not exaggerate their deeds. It criticizes Wilson for his action at the Peace Conference.

(2) L. Motta Ciaccio, *La Vita Civile.* Turin: Paravia, 1927.

This is the third volume of a series which covers ancient times, the Middle Ages, and modern times for use in the lower classes of secondary schools. The author has written a number of widely used history texts.

[49] Giovanni Gentile, *Il Fascismo al Governo della Scuola,* p. 250.

[50] It should be noted that religion is not taught in the secondary schools.

This book contains 360 pages, about 100 of them devoted to the *risorgimento,* 40 to the war, and 20 to Fascism. The author has supplemented his own text with readings from famous historians and writers and very frequently from Italian patriots. In this way considerable nationalism is introduced. Although an attempt is made to describe social and economic movements and to remain scientific, there are lapses of ardent patriotism. For example on page 306 is this passage:

"Italy did not enter the field with Germany and Austria according to the Triple Alliance, and all the Italians were glad. But this was not enough for those Italians whose hearts beat faster at the word Fatherland. Should we have looked on as indifferent spectators, as though we desired nothing on our own account, as though the Italian nation had nothing to vindicate, while the greatest war that history has ever recorded broke forth in the world, and while every nation wanted to vindicate its own rights and expand as much as possible? And what about *Italia Irredenta?* Was it not just that it should be freed from the insufferable tyranny that oppressed it? And if we did not think of freeing Italian blood, who would have thought of it in the new adjustment of Europe after the War?"

Especial attention is devoted to Roman history, and Latin is taught in the classical *ginnasi* and *licei,* girls' schools and technical institutes.[51] This is an indication of a slight renaissance of Roman studies in Italy.[52]

At the beginning of the Fascist régime about 500 of a total of 10,000 teachers were dismissed—most of them on charges of incompetence, but perhaps a score for political reasons. Both secondary school teachers and university professors are subject to the "purification" law of December 24, 1925. The Fascists have created National Fascist School Groups for secondary school-teachers and university professors, with a membership of 10,000, "the

[51] L. Severi and G. Sangiorgi, *Legislazione sull'Istruzione Media* (Turin: Paravia, 1927).

[52] Other indications are the play *Julius Caesar* by the Nationalist Fascist, Corradini; the opera *Nerone* by Boito, and open-air Greek and Roman theaters at Taormina, Syracuse, Ostia, and Verona.

spiritual militia of Fascism in the field of national culture."[53]

8. *Universities.*—In general what is true of the importance of secondary schools is also true of the universities. The number of students is comparatively small —45,557 in the year 1925–26, including both students and those attending classes without working for credit.[54] This number was distributed among twenty state and five private universities. The Fascists have made a slight attempt to control university education by instituting state examinations for degrees.[55] It should also be noted that the rectors of the universities are appointed by the state and that aside from their administrative duties they are to act as local inspectors.[56] Furthermore, professors are named by the state after competitive examinations, and are required to swear an oath of allegiance before their appointments are confirmed.[57] On the other hand the universities are free to organize instruction as they see fit and they have administrative autonomy.[58]

The state has the right to appoint *libere docenti* (free instructors), not as regular professors but because of special qualifications in their respective fields. They may be transferred from university to university, and are paid by the students who attend their classes. Their function is to stimulate the regular teaching corps. In the last few years the state has taken advantage of this institution to appoint men to give lectures on Fascist doctrines.[59]

Of the university professors who held posts at the ad-

[53] Art. 3 of Statutes. Organ: *Cultura Fascista.*

[54] *Annuario Statistico Italiano* (1927), p. 77.

[55] Decree of September 30, 1923, Art. 5.

[56] G. Lorio, *Diritto Amministrativo* (Milan: Hoeple, 1928), p. 399.

[57] Lupi, *La Riforma Gentile*, pp. 129–32.

[58] Lupi, *op. cit.*, pp. 127–29.   [59] Lupi, *op. cit.*, pp. 132–34.

vent of Fascism very few have actually been discharged and several who are known to be opponents of the Régime have been tolerated on account of their scholarship. Nevertheless, pressure has been brought to bear on some; either miserable treatment has forced them to resign or threats of discharge have made them keep their opposition under a bushel. As far as the students are concerned they are free to have whatever views they please but Fascism attempts to take them under its wing. There is in every university town and in almost all large cities a Fascist university group which pays allegiance to a central office at the party's headquarters in Rome. This organization serves as a university social center, organizes sporting events, and gives the students certain privileges—financial aid in case of need, medical aid, and reductions in railway fares and other public services. At the present time there are 27,000 members, almost all Italian students.

At the time of the reform there was an attempt to reduce the number of state universities to ten,[60] but this was not done although the state has concentrated its financial support on just ten institutions, slight help being given to the others. Instead of a reduction in the number of universities, there has been an increase of four; two institutes of higher studies became universities (Milan and Florence), and a new university has been founded at Bari, and a Catholic institution has been opened at Milan.[61]

Fascism has found its greatest university support in courses of political science and philosophy. The faculties of political science of the Universities of Rome, Pavia, Padua, Perugia, and the Superior Institute of Economic and Social Science at Florence are centers of Fascist thought and training. It is in these institutions that the

[60] Gentile, *Il Fascismo al Governo della Scuola*, pp. 198–99.

[61] Lupi, *op. cit.*, pp. 124 ff.

employees of the central, local, and colonial administration, diplomatists, consuls, vice-consuls, *Podestà,* the organizers and directors of syndicates and corporations,
and journalists are trained. Fascism has recognized the
importance of thoroughly trained men in the law and philosophy of the new order.

As an example of the courses that are given let us take
the University of Rome. Here the official professors give,
among others, courses in "comparative public law," "internal public law," and the "general doctrine" of the
state; and the *libere docenti* give courses in "syndicalist
law," "the outline for a theory of the state," and "general
theory of the state." That the Fascist leaders did not
think the existing institutions efficient was indicated by
their founding a Fascist Faculty of Political Science at
Perugia in 1928.[62] In a pamphlet issued by the Fascist
Faculty are to be found these statements:

> The Faculty which has been created fulfils a great need of the
> régime. Fascism, having become national and having synthesized the
> historical character of Italian civilization, has need of a methodical
> study of its doctrine and its political, economic and juridical institu-
> tions by the young men who enter administrative, syndicalist, or cor-
> porative, diplomatic or colonial careers.[63]

> The State which the Duce is creating and forming every day and
> every hour, must have in its arteries—in the lowest and the highest
> positions—the sentiment and consciousness, as well as the science, of
> Fascism. For this reason, according to the wish of the Duce, gradu-
> ates of the Fascist Faculty will be given preference in the various ad-
> ministrative, syndicalist, diplomatic, and colonial positions.[64]

It should also be noted that at Perugia there is a summer
school for foreigners founded in 1925, to spread Italian
culture and Fascist political ideas. Every year a series of

[62] Decree of October 23, 1927.

[63] *La Facoltà Fascista di Scienze Politiche* (Perugia: Bartelli, 1928), p. 8.

[64] *Ibid.,* p. 10.

lectures are given by leading Fascists, Mussolini himself having taken part in the first year.

Fascist ideas are also studied and taught by intellectuals at two important Fascist institutions founded in 1925—the Fascist University of Bologna and the National Fascist Institute of Culture, located at Rome but having branches in almost all the large cities of Italy. These are not universities in the real sense of the word, but *athenei,* somewhat similar to chautauqua. Gentile is responsible for the creation of both institutions, and their propaganda is charged with his idealistic conception of the state. Propaganda is carried on by means of lecture courses in the winter months, the maintenance of reading-rooms containing Fascist books and reviews, and the publication of books and reviews. The official organ of the Fascist University at Bologna is the *Vita Nova* and that of the Fascist Institute at Rome, *Leonardo.* These institutions receive state support. Although they are in their infancy they have made their influence felt, having attracted a great many young intellectuals.

In 1927 the Italian Academy at Rome was founded, obviously patterned after the French Academy. The famous Villa Farnesina was purchased as its seat. Early in 1929 the first members were announced. They were for the most part physical scientists; the names of many distinguished men in literature, philosophy, and social science (men like Benedetto Croce) were conspicuous for their absence.

CHAPTER VI

MILITARY TRAINING

1. *Fascism and militarism.—Libro e moschetto, Fascista perfetto* (a book and a musket, a perfect Fascist) : Benito Mussolini has defined an ideal Fascist with this phrase, which implies the fundamentally military nature of Fascism. There is much in common between Fascism and militarism. Both teach absolute obedience to superiors; both preach subordination of individual interests to the interests of the collective whole; both are based on an intense love for the nation and an interest in the defense and propagation of her prestige and power. Born as a war party and thriving on its military exploits, Fascism has naturally continued to exhibit a military spirit and to lay prime stress on the military organization of the state.

The importance of the Fascist emphasis on the military spirit can hardly be understood without an appreciation of the situation out of which Fascism arose. During the height of the Socialist and Communist revolts (1919–20) everything military and everything that had anything to do with the war was openly condemned. The red flag was commonly displayed in place of the tricolor; war veterans were publicly abused; soldiers and police were insulted, and many of them were killed. Frequently a trolley car would refuse to run when a policeman or soldier boarded it. Children threw stones and women threw water, bottles, and other objects out of their windows at passing uniformed men. Far from tolerating any memorials and devotions to the war heroes the populace reviled them in every way possible. Patriotism and war were

110

held to be the chief causes of the economic hardships which followed the war, and consequently everything that was allied with the national state was an object of persecution.

Against this background of disillusionment the *arditi* and Fascists arose to reassert patriotism. No doubt the still vivid memory of those "dark years" is a potent factor in keeping alive what might otherwise seem a puerile insistence on sentimental forms of nationalistic enthusiasm. Certainly the revolution in the temper of public sentiment in Italy from 1919 to 1925 is a remarkable phenomenon of "crowd psychology."

2. *Military legislation and expenditure.*—The entire period of the Fascist Régime has been dotted with important military legislation aimed not merely at rehabilitating the Italian army and navy but at reviving in the nation an interest and pride in military prowess. Of special significance are the Laws of January 11, 1923 and June 8, 1925, which provided for the mobilization of all the forces of the nation in case of war, and the Law of March 11, 1926, which provided for a reorganization of the army and revived centralized control under a chief-of-staff. The new laws of tactics approved by Mussolini, May 22, 1928, are of great importance from a technical point of view. Italy's increasing military expenditures are just one more proof of Fascist militarism.

TABLE IV

MILITARY EXPENDITURES[*]

ACTUAL EXPENDITURES IN THOUSANDS OF LIRE

1924–25	4,036,223
1925–26	4,731,954

ESTIMATED EXPENDITURES IN THOUSANDS OF LIRE

1926–27	4,897,208
1927–28	4,956,740

3. *Fascist military training.*—The Fascists, realizing the importance of military service for creating a patriotic

state of mind, have established a highly developed system of training. It begins at the age of eight and continues until eighteen for those boys who enter the Fascist juvenile organizations, *Balilla* and *Avanguardia*.[1] They are given a sound physical education and are taught the elements of military drill and modern warfare. At the age of eighteen these boys pass automatically into the Fascist party and militia and are given rifles as the symbols of their formal induction into the armed forces of the nation. For non-Fascist boys the state has created special courses of military instruction. In the school year 1927–28 there were 3,744 such classes, with 222,864 boys enrolled.[2] In every case the instructors of the youth are officers in the Fascist militia and hence faithful supporters of the Régime and ardent teachers of nationalism. A speech by Mussolini to the Avanguardisti on October 28, 1926, at the Colosseum in Rome gives an indication of the indoctrination of militaristic patriotism which goes on. "You are at the sunrise of life. You are the hope of the Fatherland. You are above all the army of tomorrow. From this moment you must live every instant of your lives with faith in the destinies of the Nation."

At the age of twenty-one[3] the young Italian is called to the army—a service which is obligatory and offers no exceptions. Students may postpone this service until their twenty-sixth year and others until their twenty-third year if they can provide legitimate reasons. Even Italian emigrants are required to undergo this training if they return to Italy before having reached the age of 32.[4] If they

---

[1] See chap. x.   [2] *Popolo d'Italia,* March 22, 1928.

[3] The Fascists have changed the age from twenty to twenty-one because it was thought that a youth of twenty was not strong enough to endure the rigors of military service. On military service see the Laws of December 4, 1911, January 7, 1923, October 15, 1925, and August 5, 1927.

[4] Law of March 25, 1926.

return after this age they are liable to service if their "class" is mobilized. On the other hand it should be noted that the service of natives in the colonies is voluntary. Native troops in the service number approximately 34,-750. The legal length of service is eighteen months, but as a matter of practice few men serve the entire period, an attempt being made in this way to reduce the budget for national defense. Those boys who have successfully passed the courses of premilitary training are entitled to a reduction of three months and some of these (about 50,-000) who have families to support or who have brothers in the army are required to serve only six months, while still others in very exceptional circumstances have this period reduced to three months. The result of such a system is that every year about 220,000 new men are called to arms, 325,000 serving during the summer months and 150,000 during the winter.[5]

Once under arms the young men soon fall into the swing of military life. They find themselves in close contact with professional soldiers and noncommissioned officers and are soon taught the traditions of the Italian army. Young men who are seamen in civil life usually serve in the navy, those with very special training, in the air force. Their new uniforms give the soldiers a feeling of superiority which is augmented by the laudatory attention of the civil population—especially the women. Marching to military music and parading on patriotic holidays and other festivals tend to lift the soldier into the realm of sentimental patriotism. Aside from these nationalistic by-products of military life, soldiers undergo a very definite patriotic education. Officers are instructed

[5] General Ugo Cavallero, *Discorso sulle Nuove Leggi Riguardanti la Riorganizzazione dell'Esercito,* delivered at the Chamber of Deputies, January 29, 1926 (Rome: Libreria dello Stato, 1926), p. 12.

to keep alive among their men "the sentiment of duty and of military honor, the spirit of sacrifice and affection for the Nation, King, and Dynasty."[6] They are to teach them that:

> All the duties of a soldier are based on one principle . . . . the necessity of the use of force for the defense of the honor and independence of the nation, of the national laws and institutions. The necessity of the use of force requires the subordination of all individual wills which make up the army to the supreme will of the command—unity of action and of force, unity of direction and of command.[7]

> In battle the soldier must never retreat from his post unless expressly ordered to do so; attentive to commands, he must execute them promptly, fire his companions by his example, ... go first where the danger is greatest, shield his superiors with his own body, and bravely face every danger of being wounded or killed with the conviction that of all the beautiful and glorious acts which may do honor to mankind none equals that of death for the Fatherland.[8]

The soldier must learn to respect the flag with a religious reverence. For him it is "the symbol of military honor, of the spirit of union and sacrifice. It reminds him of the War record of his corps or regiment. . . . . Those to whom the flag is entrusted must consider it glorious to lose their lives rather than to cede to the enemy this symbol of military honor."[9]

Aside from this prescribed nationalist instruction all military handbooks are filled with nationalist propaganda. One of the most widely used has a chapter on the Great War from which the following quotations are taken:

> Despite the arrival of vast numbers of Americans in France, the end of the War did not seem possible in 1918. Again it was Italy who turned the tide (and this time decisively) of the War. October 24 the entire Italian army charged for the final blow, and in a furious

---

[6] *Regolamento di Disciplina Militare per il Reale Esercito* (Milan, L. Di G. Pirola, 1927), p. 154.

[7] *Op. cit.*, pp. 155–56.   [8] *Op. cit.*, p. 25.   [9] *Op. cit.*, p. 26.

battle of eleven days finally clutched Austria's throat and beat her
into a lifeless mass. . . . . Only Italy of all the nations engaged in
the War had the satisfaction and pride of winning the field with
sword in hand. . . . . Every Italian recalling our glorious history,
which has no equal, must believe that our Fatherland has a still higher destiny to be preëminent and splendid in everything, and must passionately wish to contribute with all his force of heart, mind, and body
to the grandeur of our common Mother, so beautiful and so noble.[10]

The entire Italian military system is based, so far as
the ordinary soldier is concerned, on love for the nation.
His service is a great economic sacrifice, for he is paid
only forty centesimi (a little over two cents) a day. Soldiers are, of course, given their food, clothing and lodg-
ing and a small bonus when they do extra service, long
marches, and so on.[11] Despite the excellence of his work
and the bravery of his conduct the soldier receives no
material rewards. The only recognition for extraordinary service is praise or military decoration. National
loyalty is the only motive (aside from fear of punishment) for the endurance of the sacrifices required under
the present system.

Upon the conclusion of the formal period of training
the men are organized into reserves ready for immediate
mobilization for the defense of the nation. Theoretically
they are liable to calls for supplementary training but as
a matter of economy this service is not required. That
they may always be fit for military work the state maintains seven hundred rifle ranges throughout the country
and encourages her citizens to make use of them. The
physical development of civilians is cared for by a host
of sporting clubs and a new national organization, *Dopo-*

[10] Lieutenant Colonel D. Odello, *Il Libro per il Corporale di Fanteria*
(Florence: Carpigiani and Zipoli), pp. 11, 13–14.

[11] See *Prontuario pel Pagamento delle Competenze Spettanti agli Ufficiali di Tutte le Armi e Corpi* (Rome: Libreria dello Stato, 1927), p. 8.

lavoro.[12] Thanks to this system the ordinary Italian may always be prepared for immediate mobilization.

The military requirements of the Fascist state are not, however, limited to personal military service. The Great War amply demonstrated that a state must throw every ounce of its strength into the balance if it is to be victorious. The Fascists realized this and one of their first military reforms was to provide for civil mobilization in case of war. The Decree of January 11, 1923, provided for a Supreme Commission of Defense under which was organized a Committee for Civil Mobilization. Italy was divided into seven zones and army, navy, and air force experts (industrial observers) were appointed to determine the manner in which every industry might be organized for military purposes in case of war. In order that Italy may develop those industries which manufacture military materials the state and all military organizations are required to purchase Italian goods even though they cost 10 per cent more than foreign goods.[13] Every nonmilitary ministry is required to keep up to date a detailed plan for the organization in wartime of that phase of national life (agriculture, public education, justice, etc.) in which it is concerned.[14] If Italy mobilizes, all citizens, both male and female, and all organizations are obliged to come to the moral and material defense of the nation and submit to war discipline. The state has the right to requisition the individual or collective services of all Italians, of their syndicates, their property, their inventions, etc., for the defense of the country.[15] In the next war the entire nation—her industry, agriculture, universities, the

---

[12] See pp. 182–4.

[13] Law of February, 1926, No. 216. If domestic goods are more than 10 per cent higher than foreign goods purchases may be made abroad.

[14] Law of June 18, 1925.   [15] Law of June 18, 1925.

press, everything—will be forced to contribute to the struggle. The "armed nation" has come into its own in Italy.

For such a system one must have able leaders. The training of the officers to whose command the defense of the nation is intrusted is very important. Mussolini has excellently phrased the problem: "When the nation intrusts her sons to other men, she must have full confidence in these men." The Fascists have made especial efforts to provide competent officers both from a technical and a patriotic point of view. There are in Italy, as in other European nations, military families who hand down from father to son the military tradition. The sons of these families usually begin their military training in one of the two state secondary military schools at Naples and Rome. Having graduated from these institutions they go for a three years' course to one of the military universities—Modena for infantry and cavalry, Turin for artillery and engineering, or Leghorn for the navy— where they are joined by other young men who have decided upon a military career. Upon the completion of their studies in these schools they become second lieutenants and are sent to schools where they may put their knowledge into practice. These courses last one year for those in the infantry and cavalry, and two years for the artillery and engineers. There are also three central military schools at Cività-Vecchia to enable older officers to keep pace with the development of military science. Finally there is the School of War at Turin, a three years' course for those men who are to hold the highest offices in the army. In this way the officers in active service receive their training. In case of war, however, their number would be very inadequate and hence there is a host of reserve officers. Since 1927 every graduate of a secondary

school is required during his period of service to enter one
of the reserve officers' training schools. There are twelve
of them, one for each of the ten army corps in Italy and
one in Sicily and one in Sardinia. Over 6,000 boys go
through this training every year.[16] Noncommissioned officers also receive training in army corps schools, although a great many of those who are in active service
are professional soldiers, having been promoted from the
ranks.

This being in general the framework of the system for
training officers it remains to notice the spirit which per-
vades their ranks. The Italian officer is in a way the
spoiled child of the nation. His smart uniform and neat
sword make him the mark of admiration of all. Special
effort is made to keep him on a high social level, although
his salary is not great. A second lieutenant receives from
7,000 to 11,600 lire plus bonuses that may amount to
3,240 lire; a captain, 11,600 to 13,700 plus bonuses of a
maximum of 3,960 lire; and a colonel 17,800 to 20,500
plus bonuses up to 5,280 lire.[17] If an officer desires to
marry, his prospective wife must be approved by the Ministry of War,[18] and since 1926 if the marriage takes place
the officer is given a military dowry.[19] From a nationalist
point of view officers must be impeccable. Only ardent
patriots can give the troops the nationalist training described above. For this reason officers themselves all during their periods of training receive an indoctrination of
nationalist ideas. At the same time an intensive campaign
is carried on among officers to secure their support of the
Fascist Régime. In the spring of 1928 Turati, secretary

---

[16] Fulvio Zugaro, "Il Fascismo e l'Esercito," in *Civiltà Fascista,* p. 536.

[17] *Prontuario pel Pagamento delle Competenze Spettanti agli Ufficiali di
tutte le Armi e Corpe* (Rome: Libreria dello Stato, 1925), pp. 4–5.

[18] Law of June 25, 1911.   [19] Law of March 11, 1926.

of the Fascist party, concluded a series of speeches to the
various military schools with a forceful address to the
cadets at Turin. "All that I have said to you is of a political nature: it is politics as we practice it; politics from
which no one is able to keep aloof, least of all soldiers who
are the defenders and exalters of the Fatherland; racial
politics by which an entire people of artisans and soldiers
becomes an army under the orders of the King, of the
Duce, and of Italy." And if officers remain cold to the nationalist appeals which are directed at them, a new Fascist law makes it easy to dismiss them from the service.[20]

4. *Special armed corps.*—There are in Italy several
special corps which contribute to the country's defense—
and to its picturesque character. There are the Royal
Carabinieri, composed of men picked from the army,
whose purpose it is to maintain internal order. In case of
economic, social, or political trouble it is they who are in
theory the ones to maintain order. Dressed in long blue
coats, wearing cocked hats and white gloves, carrying
long swords, and parading with crossed arms, they look
like actors from a comic opera and are about as efficient.
There are some 60,000 of them with 1,246 officers. Stationed two by two all over Italy, even in the smallest ham-
lets, they serve to carry to the remotest corners of the nation the symbol of the state's control. Then there are the
twelve regiments of Bersaglieri, wearing masses of green-
black feathers on their caps. Their function has traditionally been to perform the most arduous duties of rec-
onnoitering and charging. In 1924 they were organized
into a bicycle corps. There are also the Alpine troops
with little feathers in the bands of their soft felt hats.
They are especially trained to serve in the Alps, to cope

[20] Law of March 11, 1926, Art. 75. See also Fulvio Zugaro, "Il Fascismo
e l'Esercito," in *Civiltà Fascista*, p. 534.

with the dangers and difficulties of mountain warfare. The King's Guards, composed of the tallest men in Italy, wear special helmets resembling those of the Roman soldiers. And there are the Royal Financial Guards—customs and tax-police—whose uniforms resemble those of the Alpini. Due to the fact that they are stationed on the frontiers they serve as cover troops in case of attack. In 1926 there were 30,000 of them, and they superintended the collection of taxes amounting to 11 billion lire.[21]

5. *The militia.*—But most striking of all these corps is the Fascist Voluntary Militia, the strong arm of the Fascist party.[22] This organization is the direct outgrowth of the Black Shirts who marched on Rome in 1922 and seized the reins of government by a show of force. It was only natural that a party which believed in direct action should insure its position by a military institution composed of trustworthy members. Immediately after the march on Rome Mussolini demobilized all the Fascist forces and many of the opposition hoped this would be the end of the Black Shirts. But Mussolini promptly announced that no one would be allowed to tamper with the militia and hinted that in some way or other it would be made a permanent military force of the state. In February, 1923, the militia was definitely established as a legitimate "political police force" and attached to the Ministry of the Interior. The theory was that it took the place of the small body of Royal Guards which Nitti had created in the post-war emergency and which Mussolini abolished. Mussolini explained that it was not fitting that

[21] For an account of these various corps see the *Almanacco delle Forze Armate* (1927), pp. 196–201, 259–66, 266–75, 725–35.

[22] Vittorio Verné, *La Milizia Nazionale* (Rome: Maglione and Strini, 1925); Enrico Bazan, "La Milizia Volontaria per la Sicurezza Nazionale," in *Civiltà Fascista;* and *Almanacco delle Forze Armate* (1927), pp. 735–57. The militia has its own weekly newspaper, *Milizia Fascista.*

a volunteer army obviously in the service of the party should be headed by the king. However, continued opposition induced him in 1924 to make the militia take the oath of loyalty to the king and thus to constitute one of the regular armed forces of the state. The theory of this step was that Italy needed an organized form of premilitary and postmilitary training to keep the youth of the nation constantly accustomed to the nation's services.

The army, however, did not adjust itself to the militia so easily. Before the march on Rome the army had, on the whole, exercised at least a benevolent neutrality and in some cases positive co-operation with the Black Shirts. General Diaz was Mussolini's first minister of war and other regular army officers entered the Fascist government. But friction soon developed, the following being the chief causes:

(1) It was an open secret that the Fascists were using army funds for the militia and were gradually shifting the best rifles and new equipment from the regular army to the militia.

(2) Militia officers were treated with greater respect by Fascists than the corresponding ranks of regular army officers, and on the other hand the regulars treated the militia with considerable condescension: General Diaz, for example, flatly refused to accept militia officers on equal terms with regulars. This mutual jealousy and rivalry grew until on several occasions, notably in the fall of 1924, open hostility between the two organizations was manifested.

(3) The Fascists permitted regular army officers to leave the army and join the militia with a raise in rank and salary.

(4) The continued violences and illegalities of Fas-

cist squads openly sponsored by the head of the militia, Italo Balbo, scandalized the army.

These sources of friction have been gradually eliminated. Balbo was forced to resign and on October 9, 1926, Mussolini assumed personal command of the militia. A decree made it impossible for army officers to better their standing by joining the militia. In general the militia gradually became more orderly and assumed a more genuinely military bearing, and on the other hand the general staff of the army was "purified." On the whole, relations between the militia and the army are now fairly cordial.

The rôle of the militia has now become clearer and its activities are more in harmony with the theory that it is primarily a premilitary training school of national service. Since January 6, 1927, the doors of the party and hence of the militia have been closed except by the process of promotion into it from the Avanguardia. Promotion into the militia is celebrated annually by a huge festival —the *Leva Fascista*—on the Sunday nearest March 23.

The members of the militia remain in civil life unless called to arms in case of trouble or for active police work. They receive no pay except while on active duty and during the few days of each year when the entire militia is mobilized. They eat at home when possible and buy their own uniforms. On this account they are relatively not at great expense to the government. The service has a budget of 50,000,000 lire. But in the popular imagination the heavy burden of taxation is not infrequently blamed on the militia. In discussing the high cost of living, people can often be heard of remark, "It costs something to support *two* armies."

Aside from protecting the Fascist Régime from a counter-revolution, the militia soldiers serve as a relief organization in case of disaster. In a way they supplement the service of the Carabinieri but they are frequently more efficient and command more respect. They police trains to see that they run on time and that both personnel and passengers keep their feet off the seats and remain politically correct; they furnish instructors for premilitary education, and in case of war they will probably serve as assault troops. Recently the duties of the militia were extended to include the protection of forests, the policing of the border, of ports, and of the postal, telephone, and telegraph services. These functions of the militia are still in their infancy.

The militia is organized on the plan of the ancient Roman army. Its units, with the corresponding regular army units in parentheses, are as follows: squad (squad), maniple (platoon), century (company), cohort (battalion), legion (regiment), zone (division). There are fifteen zones exclusive of the colonies, and at present there are 130 legions, exclusive of 2 legions in Lybia and exclusive of the special militias (railroads, ports, forests, etc.). There are two general divisions of the militia; the first division is composed of men who can be mobilized at a moment's notice and the second division of those who, because of their occupation, residence, or age, can be called only in emergencies. The number of militiamen in active service varies considerably from time to time. Of the officers, about 700 are now in active, continuous service and about 7,000 are in reserve. About 250,000 Black Shirts were mobilized for the march on Rome and this number is being maintained, but now only a small fraction of the total is on active duty. There are 25,000 on duty as railroad police (being regular railroad employees) and about 3,000 border police. There are also several colonial legions of militia.

With their black shirts, ties, and caps (fez), and their smart uniforms, which resemble those of the Alpine troops, the militiamen are living symbols of Fascist authority and conspicuous embodiments of militant nationalism.

6. *Army associations.*—Another important agent of military training and enthusiasm is the National Union of Reserve Officers *(L'Unione Nazionale degli Ufficiali in Congedo),* founded in 1926 by the union of various small associations of officers. Its purpose is to maintain a military spirit among reserve officers and to furnish them with the latest information concerning military affairs. Although a comparatively young association, the Union has become the most important society of officers and a new force in the patriotic militant life of the nation. Similar organizations exist for almost every branch of the Italian military establishment—the National Association of Infantry, the National Association of the Grenadiers of Sardinia, the National Association of Bersaglieri, of Alpine Troops, of the Cavalry, and of the Carabinieri— all contributing to the military spirit of the country.[23]

Besides these there are the military Orders of Knights: the Supreme Order of Santissimi Annunziata, which dates from 1363 (it has only twenty members, who are chosen from among Italians who have distinguished themselves in the military or civil life of the nation) ; the Equestrian Order of SS. Maurizio and Lazzaro, founded in 1434, composed of both civil and military personages;

[23] *Almanacco delle Forze Armate* (1927), pp. 764–75.

the Military Order of Savoy, founded in 1815 by Victor
Emmanuel I when he returned to his estates; the order of
the Crown of Italy, founded by Victor Emmanuel II in
1868 to celebrate the annexation of Venetia to the kingdom of Italy; the Institution of the Blue Ribbon, a creation of Fascism, founded in 1923 and presided over by
Benito Mussolini.[24]

7. *Navy propaganda.*—In addition to the army propaganda diffused by all these associations there is also that
for the navy. This is the active concern of the Italian
Naval League.[25]

Vast is the program of the League, very distant its radiant goal,
but with faith and tenacity it shall be reached. A maritime program
cannot help being successful among Italians, for it will reveal the
sacred mission of the new Italy in the world. Our Nation must regain
the civil primacy of the world by means of the sea as it was won by
Rome and the glorious maritime Republic. Maritime expansion, destined to maintain that political independence for us which must obtain our economic independence, is a question of vital interest to us.
On it depends whether or not we shall be a great nation.

Faithful to the Régime and imbued with the ideas expressed in the declaration quoted above, the League carries its message to the schools by means of lectures, prizes,
and pamphlets; to its members by printed propaganda,
the bimonthly review, and sea voyages, and to the general
public by every modern means of propaganda. It carries
on special work among seamen, furnishing them maritime information and financial aid for sailors' widows and
orphans. In this work its task is lightened by the support
of another organization, the Italian Maritime Union,

[24] For more details concerning these orders see R. E. Ceschina, *Gli Ordini
Equestri del Regno d'Italia* (Milan: Ceschina, 1925); and *Almanacco delle
Forze Armate* (1927), pp. 763 ff.

[25] Founded, 1899. Headquarters: Via Giustiniani 5, Rome. Organ:
L'Italia Marinara (bimonthly).

which is a fraternal and patriotic society of sailors, with headquarters in Milan.[26]

The most effective form of naval propaganda at present comes directly from the government. As a corollary to Fascist imperialism[27] comes the inevitable emphasis on maritime power. This has taken the following general forms:

(1) An emphasis on the Roman power in the Mediterranean, the *Mare Nostrum* idea: It is constantly being pointed out that Italy must once more become the predominant power on the Mediterranean in order to carry out her need of "expansion." In October, 1926, for example, Mussolini announced an "academic lecture" at the University of Perugia. This lecture bore the title "Ancient Rome on the Seas" and it purported to demonstrate that Rome owed her power in large part to her maritime supremacy, both mercantile and military. This lecture has been given wide circulation and its theme even wider.

(2) For the present the emphasis is on the merchant marine rather than on the navy: By liberal subsidies and extensive advertising the government is encouraging Italian companies to compete with other nations for the trans-Atlantic traffic, especially for that with South America.

(3) The diplomatic policy of eastward expansion by way of the African colonies, Egypt, the Arab states, and Syria is to be supported by the development of marine trade routes with these countries: The chief Mediterranean ports are being enlarged, notably Bari.

(4) Mussolini and other Fascist officials are constant-

[26] For information on maritime affairs see the *Annuario Navale* compiled by the Navy League.

[27] See chap. iii.

ly praising the maritime occupations and encouraging the development of ship-building and the training of sailors as the most promising outlet for Italy's surplus labor.

8. *Aviation enthusiasm.*—The most popular and pressing military appeal at present is, of course, to aviation. The enthusiasm for aviation is quite general in all countries and is not predominantly military. What is characteristic of Italy, however, is that the government itself has taken the lead and is openly encouraging aviation for military motives rather than for commerce or sport.

Shortly after the March on Rome, that is, March 28, 1923, a separate Ministry of Aviation and an independent Royal Aeronautic Corps were created. On May 4, 1925, a royal decree announced an ambitious program of aerial construction aimed to give Italy by 1930 a total of 182 squads of aeroplanes, 6 dirigibles, and 8 enlarged military aviation stations. This represents an enormous effort at expansion when compared with the present force of 91 squads, 2 dirigibles, and 7 aviation stations, and it gives practical force to Mussolini's repeated rhetorical statements that by 1935 Italy must be able to darken her skies with the wings of her planes.

The recent exploits of Italian military aviators are too well known the world over to call for description here, but what is not generally known is the enormous excitement and patriotic passion which they arouse in Italy. It is but a few years ago that the poet, d'Annunzio, tried to fire the popular imagination with his love for "the wings of Italy" and his romantic gestures toward aviation; but today even d'Annunzio seems calm amid the wave of wild enthusiasm. In Italy, I repeat, this aviation craze has a decidedly military flavor and importance, for the only .

serious and organized aviation is controlled by the government and operated by military officers. Thus there is every inducement imaginable to draw young men into this branch of military service.[28]

[28] Information concerning the Italian military establishments may be had from the following sources: *Almanacco delle Forze Armate* (Rome: Tipografica del Senato, 1927); Vittorio Giglio, *Milizie ed Eserciti d'Italia* (Milan: Ceschina, 1927); *Annuaire Militaire* (Geneva: League of Nations, 1928); Fulvio Zugaro, *Il Fascismo e l'Esercito;* Maffio Maffii, *Marina e Fascismo;* Italo Balbo, *Il Fascismo e l'Aviazione,* and Enrico Bazan, "La Milizia Volontaria per la Sicurezza Nazionale," in *La Civiltà Fascista* (Turin: U.T.E.T., 1928); and U.P.E., *Opere e Leggi del Regime Fascista* (Rome: Tipografica Italica, 1927), pp. 2554. Military newspaper: *Le Forze Armate,* published twice a week. Officers' review: *Esercito e Nazione.*

CHAPTER VII
THE BUREAUCRACY

1. *The moral and economic status of civil servants.* —In Italy the employees of the state are no longer considered mere non-political beings whose permanence in office should be guaranteed by all political parties. This English theory of civil service has been cast overboard. Fascism teaches that the public employee cannot serve the state and at the same time oppose the government, for the government and state blend into each other. Consequently, if the civil servant is opposed to the government, he is opposed to the state.[1] It logically follows that under the new order the public functionary is not only the performer of certain duties for which he receives a stipend but also a political force and even an agent of propaganda in whom the Fascist state may find a servant for the support and promulgation of its doctrines. It is for these reasons that the bureaucracy plays a unique rôle in Italian civic training.

Public employees are divided into three grades according to the educational requirements for their positions: those having university degrees; those having superior secondary school diplomas, and those having only an inferior secondary school education. They are further divided into thirteen grades according to the positions they hold.[2] They are appointed after competitive exam-

[1] *Bollettino Parlementare,* No. 2 (Rome: Camera dei Deputati, June, 1927), p. 65.

[2] *Ordinamento Gerarchio delle Amministrazione dello Stato* (Rome: Libreria dello Stato, 1913), p. 2. A handy collection of laws pertaining to public employees is *Codice della Burocracia* (Rome: Camera dei Deputati, 1926).

inations, preference being given, other things equal, to decorated war veterans.[3] Once appointed the employee is placed on trial for six months,[4] and if satisfactory is given a permanent position. In every ministry there is a Council of Administration which gives every employee in the first five "grades" an annual mark according to his merits, and promotions are based upon these marks. Above the fifth grade merit is judged by the Council of Ministers and promotion is dependent on this judgment.[5]

Public employees receive salaries varying from 4,200 lire (plus bonuses for high cost of living, active service, traveling, etc., which may amount to 2,985 lire) to 46,000 (plus 13,000 for active service) and have the advantage of pensions varying with the periods of service.[6] These figures represent, in terms of real cost, a lowering of 30 to 50 per cent of the pre-war level, but they are probably a little higher than the level of 1920. An employee ordinarily works seven hours a day, but not even the eight-hour day is legally established.

2. *Fascist legislation governing state employees.*—From the moment that the public employee expresses a desire to enter the service of the state, his political views play an important part in his career. In order to secure an appointment he must give proof of having led a correct civil, moral, and political life.[7] The employee does not have the right to strike[8] but the state reserves the right to remove employees.[9] A very important Fascist law permits the state to discharge civil servants who "by

[3] Decree of November 11, 1923, Arts. 3 and 21.   [4] *Ibid.,* Art. 17.

[5] Decree of December 30, 1923, Arts. 11, 12, 13, 19 ff., and Decree of July 8, 1925.

[6] *Il Pubblico Impiego,* May 15, 1928, p. 3.

[7] *Disposizioni sullo Stato Giuridico degl'Impiegati Civili dell'Amministrazione dello Stato;* Decree of December 30, 1923, Art. 1–6.

[8] Decree of December 30, 1923, Art. 46.   [9] *Ibid.,* Art. 47.

reason of acts committed either in or out of office do not give full guarantee of a complete faith in their duties or who make themselves incompatible with the general political aims of the government."[10]

For reasons of reorganization, economy, and politics the personnel of the state, both civil and military, which in 1920 was 400,000 and by the first of July, 1921, had increased to 591,053, was decreased to 512,435 by January, 1927. Of this diminution of 79,000, 60,000 were railway employees, 15,000 postal, telegraph, and telephone workers, and 4,000 civil administrators.[11] Among these administrators were employees of the various ministries. Mussolini insisted on a reduction of the personnel in all the ministries except those immediately under him. The Labor Ministry was abolished entirely. In January, 1928, the number had decreased to 506,652, representing an annual expenditure of 5,461,391,157 lire.[12]

As part of the Fascist policy of drawing all Italians under the wing of the state and of the Fascist party itself, there was founded in 1927 a General Fascist Association of Public Employees. It is open to all public servants with the exception of members of the armed forces of the state, judges, and professors of secondary schools and universities. Article 11 of the Law of April 3, 1926, prohibits their membership. Great pressure is brought to bear on all others to join. In 1927 the membership was 251,000. The association aims to aid civil servants financially by defending their interests, to provide them with information concerning their work, and to maintain a high morale among them. In the latter field it proposes to form a "firm civil and national consciousness by means

[10] Law of December 24, 1925, Art. 1.

[11] *Il Pubblico Impiego,* January 1, 1928, p. 1.

[12] *Gazzetta Ufficiale,* March 10, 1928.

of lectures, publications and every other means of propaganda capable of spreading information concerning great national problems."[13] As an example of this propaganda let us consider two articles which appeared in the Association's official bimonthly paper:

Our Association must constitute in the state's mechanism, which is the main artery of the entire nation, a strong and loyal fortress. You must realize that you do not serve Fascism simply by paying for a badge and dues, which after all are very small though necessary, but that you serve it by participating actively in the life of our Association, collaborating with its organs, overcoming daily those disgraceful petty things which still persist, and working tirelessly for the acceleration of all public services. . . . . We must continue and persevere, realizing that we are doing good work not for the interest of any individual, which, if something, is very small, but for the interest of the State and of the Italian Nation. That is the spirit![14]

The functionary of the Fascist State should be a Fascist, should be a soldier in the field of eternal combat, should work day in and day out, hour by hour, fervidly and feverishly, for the high mission which has been entrusted to him. Public functionaries should be ardent and patient instruments of an intense national life.

This our Association teaches to its members. . . . .[15]

The unique moral and political status of public employees has become all the more pronounced since the organization of the national confederations and the so-called corporate state. The basic Law of April 3, 1926, gave legal recognition and official duties to the Fascist syndicates, and at the same time provided that though public employees may form associations, such associations have no legal recognition. This implies that the new economic order defined by the Labor Charter does not apply to Associations of Public Employees. The state, as employer, is bound by no "collective contracts," its employees have no recourse to the regular labor tribunals

[13] Constitution of the Association, Art. 3. See *Il Pubblico Impiego,* March 27, 1927.

[14] April 15, 1927, p. 2.   [15] June 1, 1927, p. 2.

and have no collective rights. The right to strike is, of course, denied to all Italian employees, public and private. But the private employee by means of his syndicate and the Ministry of Corporations can engage in collective bargaining and can thus promote his professional and material interests. The public employee, on the other hand, is on the same footing as the soldier; his duties as an employee are indistinguishable from his moral obligations to his country. Hence both the state and its employees must be governed by political and moral, not by economic, considerations.

This Fascist theory of public employment is succinctly expressed by Alfredo Rocco, minister of justice, as follows:

The relations between the state and its personnel are of a very different nature, not only because the state can not be placed on the same level with the citizen whom it has engaged as its agent or employee, but also for very delicate reasons of an ethical and juridical nature. In fact, while a private individual in organizing his enterprise and guaranteeing a certain kind of treatment to his personnel is not legally obliged to take account of any other principle than his own interest, the state and other public organs, inasmuch as they are ethical organisms, must do justice to their personnel.

So true is this that at the very heart of the administration of the state and other public organs, bodies have been created intended to enforce justice for public functionaries, employees, and agents. In the legislation of the last forty years on the subject of administrative justice, the constitution of special jurisdictional bodies such as the provincial administrative commissions and the Fourth Session of the Council of State, is evidence of this particular exigency in the life of the state, which the Italian state has fully grasped and partially satisfied. I say only in part because Italian legislation on the subject of administrative justice, though it is far advanced, is certainly not yet perfect and some things still remain to be done to render full justice to the personnel of the state and other public bodies. . . . .[16]

[16] From Rocco's speech in the Chamber of Deputies in defense of the Law of April 3, 1926.

Rocco's thesis that justice is formally due to the public employee by the Fourth Session of the Council of State loses some of its force when it is remembered that in January, 1924, the Fascists had tampered with this august body. This Fourth Session had been the pride of liberalism, an independent, supreme court with authority to try the administrative acts of the government itself. Such a court, with authority over the government, naturally conflicted with Fascist theory and practice. Consequently in January, 1924, the Fourth Session was fused with the Third "in order to give administrative jurisdiction the efficiency which it lacked,"[17] but really in order to assert the supremacy of the government.

3. *Methods of maintaining the discipline and dignity of the civil service.*—Theory apart, the fact is that the public employee is at the mercy of the government. The consequence is that the dignity of a civil servant has been lowered in the popular and in his own estimation. This is, of course, just the opposite result from that aimed at by the Fascists. For the Fascist movement had taken its rise precisely at a time when everything connected with the state, especially uniformed state employees, was despised and persecuted, and one of the prime aims of Fascism was the restoration of the dignity and honor of the state.

In this situation the government is actively concerned to give what dignity it can to public service, in spite of the fact that public servants are deprived of the private and syndical rights and powers of other employees. The general techniques for achieving this aim are the following:

(1) The General Fascist Association of Public Employees, whose activities have been described in the fore-

[17] Mussolini, *La Nuova Politica,* II, 175.

going, is given as much official recognition and encouragement as possible: The director of this association, Aldo Lusignoli, makes it a point to keep in personal touch with the members of the government and party, and to publish in the association's periodical *(Il Pubblico Impiego)* compliments, speeches, and other forms of hortatory literature by prominent officials. Many prefects and other officials have ordered their subordinates to give this association all the support in their power, and several of the measures recommended by the association have received exceptionally prompt and favorable hearing.

(2) Augusto Turati and other officers of the party continually emphasize the doctrine that the bureaucracy, civil and military employees of the state, stand in a peculiarly intimate relation to the party and therefore enjoy the party's special solicitude: This solicitude of the party has a positive and a negative aspect. Negatively it takes the form of "purification." To be an employee of the state means to be a servant of the government, that is, of the Fascist Régime. Hence anyone who is not an active and whole-hearted Fascist is unfit to be a civil servant and deserves to be weeded out by the process of purification. Naturally this theory cannot be applied rigorously and instantaneously, for the government needs the technical skill of many in the bureaucracy of whose Fascist faith it cannot be too sure. Nevertheless the policy of purification means a continual pressure on all who fail to show the necessary "political and moral qualifications."

Positively the policy means that young Fascists as soon as they prove competent, and even sooner, may expect the material rewards of their faith in the form of promotion and preferment. But in addition a Fascist official, however low in rank, is invested with the dignity and prestige of the party, which makes him feel morally superior to private employees. He is apt to show this superiority in every possible way and usually receives the support of the Fascist party hierarchy.

(3) A third form of recognition has come through the Ministry of Corporations: Hardly had the supposedly voluntary and not legally recognized Association of Public Employees been formed than it was "attached" to the Ministry of Corporations though it was not embodied in the corporate organization of syndicates. Giuseppe Bottai, the minister of corporations, went out of his way to explain that "between the associations of state employees and the syndicates there is only a single difference: they have different functions; but neither the associations nor the syndicates can claim particular rights in respect to the Fascist state. The associations of state employees must be convinced that they enter into the orbit of the Corporate State with different attributes but with the same dignity enjoyed by any other syndicate."[18] Not satisfied with this recognition he went on to suggest that the servants of the state, "being freed from the petty daily struggle for wages, can dedicate themselves to an enterprise which is vaster, nobler, and more essential to the future of the Italian nation and its political formation."

How effective this moralistic technique is we shall not attempt to say, for it is impossible to generalize on the subject of temperamental differences in the face of moral appeal.

(4) We pass on to a less sentimental form of Fascist support for the bureaucracy coming from Mussolini as minister of the interior: Here we must first pause to give a general picture of the historical relations between Fas-

[18] From his speech at the Congress of Public Health Officers, Siena, September 17, 1927, published in *Il Pubblico Impiego,* October 1, 1927.

cism and the bureaucracy. The greatest factor in the demoralization of the bureaucracy during the first few years of the Fascist Régime was the overlapping of offices and confusion of responsibilities caused by the constant interference of Fascist party officials in the functions of the administration, both local and national. The overzealous Fascist officers, especially the provincial secretaries of the party, made the Revolution an excuse for interfering wherever they pleased in government affairs. The so-called "integralists," to say nothing of the Old Guard, or "1919ers," were insistent in their demand that the "old bureaucracy" be cleaned out root and branch, and that all government jobs be turned over to bonafide Fascists. The central junto of the party, itself tending to usurp the functions of the government, allowed its local and provincial officers considerable freedom and power. As a result the administration of the interior and practically all branches of the civil service were thoroughly disrupted and thrown into confusion. The Matteotti crisis brought this state of affairs to a head and induced Mussolini and the more serious Nationalist politicians to try to bring order out of chaos. Gradually the doctrine of purification was applied to overbearing party officers as well as to the non-Fascist elements in the bureaucracy, and thus gradually Mussolini got the situation under control. The institution of *podestà* and appointive municipal councils, the gradual appointment of reliable Fascists as prefects of the provinces, the strengthening of the cabinet, and a number of other administrative reforms built up a highly centralized bureaucracy under the direct control of Mussolini and his undersecretaries in the government. The culmination of this policy came in Mussolini's famous Circular to the Prefects, January, 1927, of which we give the relevant parts:

The prefect—I solemnly repeat—is the highest authority of the state in the province. He is the direct representative of the central executive power. All citizens and especially those who have the great privilege and honor of being Fascist soldiers, owe respect and obedience to the highest political representative of the Fascist Régime and they must subordinately collaborate with him so as to render his task easier. Wherever it is necessary, the prefect should stimulate and harmonize the activity of the Party in its various manifestations, but it is quite clear to all that the authority can not be run on "shares." Nor is shirking of authority or responsibility to be tolerated. A single person must be in authority. . . . .

Now that the state is armed with all means of prevention and repression, there are "residues" which must disappear. I speak of squadrism which in 1927 is simply anachronistic and sporadic, but which nevertheless reappears tumultuously in moments of public excitement. These illegalities must end. Not only those which, exploding in the poor little arrogant locations, nevertheless endanger the Régime and sow useless and dangerous seeds of rancor, but also those others which develop after serious events. . . . . Those prefects who do not act according to the above scheme will be considered vile and traitorous servants of the Fascist Régime and as such I will punish them. It is not necessary for me to add that the prefect must always tell the truth, all the truth, to the government especially when it may hurt him. . . . .

In addition to governing according to the institutional laws of the Régime the Fascist prefect must "purify" the lesser bureaucracy and indicate to the Party and to the responsible organs of the Régime the detrimental elements. The Fascist prefect should see to it that all grafters, profiteers, self-trumpeters, hot-air merchants, cowards, those infected with false political doctrines, the vain, the sowers of petty quarrels and discord, and all those who do not lead an open and public life should be removed and banished from all organizations and forces of the Régime. . . . .

The Fascist prefect is not like the prefect of democratic-liberal times. In those times the prefect was above all an electoral personage. Now that elections are no longer mentioned, the prefect can change his bearing and manner. The prefect must take all the initiatives which properly belong to the Régime or which increase its strength and prestige in the social as well as the intellectual realm. The problems which at any time press upon the population (housing, high cost of living, etc.) must be considered by the prefect. It is the prefect who must see to it that government measures (of a social nature and relating to public works) do not suffer from local complications.

Under the new administrative and corporate order it is the prefect who must be at the head of the whole life of the province and from the prefect the life of the province must receive its stimulus, coördination and direction. The prefect must consider the needs and necessities of the people even when these have no means of making themselves felt by an organization or order of the day; he must discover unexpressed needs and the too often ignored forms of wretchedness. Wherever it may be possible he must make basic moral and political improvements and show to the people that the Fascist State is not a selfish, cold, and insensible state. Without demagogy and slavishness he must do good to those who merit it. This work of assistance and sympathy must be developed particularly in respect to the new generations which are being organized in the Balilla and Avanguardia. These adolescents must be regarded as the great and splendid promise of the Fascist Italy of tomorrow.

These are your instructions. I know that you are faithful representatives of the Fascist State. Therefore you will apply them intelligently, assiduously, and faithfully.

It is perhaps not necessary to read between the lines to see that this circular was intended primarily to center complete responsibility in the prefects and thus to curtail the officiousness of party secretaries and other meddlers. On another occasion Mussolini said, "I shall hand over no prefect's scalp to a provincial secretary."

This indicates quite clearly the general trend of Fascist policy with regard to the bureaucracy. The government relies increasingly on this hand-picked completely centralized body not only to maintain public order but also by their example and administration to lay the foundations of the Fascist civic spirit of absolute devotion to the state, which constitutes the cornerstone of Fascist theory and the stumbling-block of Fascist practice.

CHAPTER VIII
THE FASCIST PARTY

1. *The one-party system.*—The relation of Fascism to other political parties has gone through the following general stages:

(1) From 1915 to 1920 the *fasci* and similar organizations were non-political: They were *fasci* (groups, bands) precisely because they believed in direct action and not in party tactics. Some of the *fasci* derived this attitude from the direct action philosophy of the syndicalists and maximalist socialists; others, from a conservative disdain for democratic institutions. The former attitude was most typically expressed by the futurist *fasci* (1918), the latter by the Nationalist Association, founded in 1910.

(2) From 1921 to 1923 the Fascists played the parliamentary game: They ran for Parliament, affiliated themselves with the Nationalist wing on the extreme Right, and, after October 28, 1922, tried to carry on a national coalition government. For a brief period a number of Nationalists, Liberals, Democrats, and Popularists took part in Mussolini's government. The Electoral Reform of 1924 and the subsequent elections were based on the idea of government by a solid majority of two-thirds (called the National List and containing various political groups besides Fascists) opposed by the minority groups, who were to be shorn of effective power but retained as instruments of criticism, advice, and deliberation.

(3) From 1924 to 1926 Fascism was forced by oppo-

sition, scandal, and intrigue to abandon this position and
stamp out all opposition: During this time Fascist candidates ran against those of other parties in local elections,
and usually won, even in traditionally hostile centers
(e.g., Palermo). The primary activity of the Fascist
party was combat, carried on in the press, in local campaigns, by patriotic celebrations and speeches, and by occasional raids and acts of violence.[1]

During this time several attempts were made by pro-
Fascist elements in other parties to rehabilitate themselves. For example, some Popularists re-entered the
Chamber of Deputies (only to be thrown out) ; some Liberals formed a National Liberal party (May, 1925),
which was willing to co-operate with the Fascist party,
but it was abolished in 1926 when all other parties and
secret societies were stamped out.

(4) Since 1926 the political dictatorship and monopoly of the Fascist party has not been seriously challenged,
for the government itself, at the instigation of the party,
has wiped out all opposition by promulgating decrees
and by various punitive measures such as personal persecution, banishment, imprisonment, and forced unemployment: Consequently the party has not been preoccupied
with the opposition parties but with internal party politics and with the cultivation of the Fascist spirit, especially among the younger generations.

This evolution of a strictly one-party system came
about by force of circumstances and not by the consistent
application of a political philosophy. The Fascist Revolution was carried out before it was thought out; hence
the justification which is usually given for the one-party
dictatorship is simply political necessity. Nevertheless
several general ideas have been developed in Italy in de-

[1] See chap. ix.

fense of this system, which it might be well to mention here, as they constitute what theoretical basis there is for the Fascist conception of civic training:

a) Italy is supposed to be in a constant state of war, either politically or economically: Her needs far exceed her resources, and hence she is compelled to fight her way among her richer neighbors. In this situation, politics must be unified and political education must consist in teaching the people the doctrine of national solidarity in the face of foreign competing powers.[2]

b) The notion of class struggle and conflicting class interests is abandoned in favor of the notion of a nation made up of interdependent producers competing with other nations: A person is a citizen in so far as he is a producer and he has rights only in so far as his production is of service to the nation. Consequently, both in economics and politics, the social order must be so constituted and so regulated as to emphasize this national co-operative union of producers.[3] The Fascists contend that no party system, and no appeal to the exclusive representation of particular groups, classes, or points of view can ever bring about an efficient *national* economy.

c) It follows that the democratic conception of citizenship, of public opinion, and political representation is completely abandoned: The theory is that under modern conditions it is impossible for a "citizen" to be informed intelligently on national issues and capable of assuming responsibility for the government. The individual person is obliged to "tend to his own business" as a producer and to intrust government to a specially trained bureaucracy *(classe dirigente)* whose sole and special business it is to govern the nation.

d) Fascism distinguishes sharply between popular

[2] See chap. iii.   [3] See chap. i.

government and representative government: It claims to be a popular government, though a dictatorship, so long as it promotes the welfare of the people as a whole and enjoys the people's loyal and disciplined obedience. It condemns traditional party government (such as the cabinet system produced in Italy) as not even a government of and by the majority, but merely a constant bickering of minorities for political privileges and special interests.

e) Various theories of the delegation of authority have been propounded by Fascist philosophers, ranging from the divine-right theory to the plebiscite theory, but they all agree that once an authority is recognized it is responsible only to the king, and the king is but the symbol for the unity of the nation.

On the basis of such ideas, it is clear that Fascism must deny categorically any rights whatsoever to any other party, actual or future. "The Régime is a closed system." It will no doubt yield some day to a successor, but while it lasts it demands undivided power.

It must not be supposed that this party dictatorship rests entirely on force. The organizations of the opposition parties, to be sure, have yielded only to force; but it is undeniable that the Fascists are able to count on a large amount of popular support and sympathy. Even among the opposition party politicians considerable numbers have yielded to the pressure and have voluntarily asked to be allowed to "co-operate." Such moves came from groups of Socialists, Popularists, and Liberals.

The drastic laws of November, 1926, banished over seven hundred political prisoners, mostly communists, to the islands, but of these more than a hundred have already been granted full or partial amnesty by Mussolini. Amnesty has also been granted to several hundred others who had been imprisoned, "admonished," or punished in some other way. These are probably symptoms that the crisis is over and that the government is to a considerable extent "popular."

2. *The party's function in the Régime.*—The really serious problem in Italy today is not the attitude of the Fascist party to other parties but the function of the party in the government. Now that the opposition parties have disappeared, the question arises, what can a single party do? One party implies another. Nor is this problem merely theoretical. The party machine has many enemies within and without the Fascist movement, and consequently at every pretext the demand is heard to abolish the party as a party. The sources of this demand are, in general, the following:

(1) The Old Guard or the "1919ers" are, most of them, of the squadrist type and never countenanced the transformation of Fascism from local *fasci* into a national political party: They have a special scorn for the party politicians because these have been overinsistent on "discipline" and have wrested control from local leaders and vested it in the party hierarchy. Finding themselves losers in the political game, the old squadrists are apt to look down upon the politicians, regarding them not only as newcomers and meddlers but as petty office-seekers who have debased the noble spirit of military Fascism and have resorted to old political tactics.

(2) A more general source of distrust comes from the widespread belief that the party is merely duplicating the offices and functions of the government, and that it is therefore not merely a useless expense but a positive nuisance, interfering with regular government officers and using underhanded methods to gain its ends: This attitude was strongest in 1924 at the time of the Matteotti affair, when the scandalous doings of the party junto

were exposed. The party was then regarded as a mill-stone about the neck of the serious and industrious Mussolini government. Since that time the contrast between party and government has been greatly diminished. The government proved less "pure" than was at first supposed and on the other hand the party was gradually purified of some of its worst elements. In general, the friction between government and party was represented by the two factions, the Federzoni Nationalist faction entrenched in the government, and the Farinacci faction (representing the local boss [ras] type, the intransigents, and the squadrists) entrenched in the party. Now that Farinacci has been succeeded by Turati as general secretary of the party, and now that Federzoni has left the Ministry of the Interior and become minister of colonies, the breach is healed and Mussolini has established a firm personal control over both party and government. But for this very reason the question is still raised: why does not Mussolini free himself from the useless party?

(3) Still a third attitude comes from liberalistic Fascists, like Gentile, who are quite willing to retain the party but want it to abandon politics and become frankly a "spiritual organization," with civic and educational functions.

(4) Then there is a group of young "aristocrats" among the Fascists, who object to the party hierarchy and its emphasis on discipline: They are quite willing to have a dictatorship by the Fascists over Italy, but they resent too much dictatorship within the ranks. The party, according to them, ought to be organized more or less democratically and flexibly, giving ample scope for individual variations and genius.[4]

[4] See for example the writings of Pellizzi, and editorials in the *Critica Fascista*.

The problem indicated by these various points of view has not been entirely solved as yet, but the general direction taken can be indicated by the following events:

(1) Mussolini made it quite clear that the party would remain as a party, not, however, to continue political conflict but to form the nucleus and training school for the governing class *(classe dirigente),* and to create an atmosphere of national discipline and patriotism for the coming generation.

(2) The duties of the party are being restricted to various philanthropic, patriotic, and social services, leaving the strictly political functions to the bureaucracy: The two documents which have definitely settled this are (*a*) Mussolini's Circular to the Prefects (discussed in chapter vii, pp. 137–39) and (*b*) the New Constitution of the Fascist party (which we shall discuss below).

(3) The party is being increasingly centralized and placed directly at Mussolini's bidding: All remnants of democracy have disappeared and control is invariably exercised according to the Fascist principle of hierarchy and discipline.

(4) The Grand Council of the party was made (1928) one of the chief organs of the government and the ultimate seat of authority.

3. *The New Constitution of the Fascist party.*— These points can be best understood through an examination of the New Constitution of the Fascist party, which was drawn up by Secretary Turati and ratified by the Grand Council, October 8, 1926.

Of the preamble we quote the following:

Fascism is a militia at the service of the nation. Its aim: to bring about the greatness of the Italian people. From its very beginnings, which coincide with the rebirth of the Italian spirit and the will to victory, Fascism has always regarded itsself as in a state of war, at first in order to overthrow those who were stifling the nation's will power; today and always to promote the power of the Italian people.

Fascism is not merely a group of Italians gathered together for the sake of a specific program attained or to be attained, but is above all a faith which has had its confessors and in whose ranks the new Italians are working as soldiers, whose energy was created by the victorious War and by the succeeding strife between the nation and the anti-nation.

The Party is the essential aspect of these forces and the operation of the Party is fundamentally indispensable for the vitality of the Régime. . . . .

Being opposed to dogmatic formulas and rigid principles, Fascism feels that victory lies in the possibility of continually renewing itself. Fascism lives today in the service of the future and looks to the new generations as to the forces destined to attain all the goals to which we have dedicated ourselves.

The organization and hierarchy, however, without which there can be no discipline of energies nor education of the people, must be illuminated and guided from on top, where there is a comprehensive view of powers, duties, functions, and merits.

The seat of authority and controlling body of the Fascist party is the Grand Council of the nation and of the state, formerly known as the Grand Council of the Fascist party. It is constituted as follows: the head of the government (president); the quadrumviri of the march on Rome; the president of the Senate and the president of the Chamber; the ministers of state; the under-secretary of state; the head of the militia; the secretary of the Fascist party and those who held that position prior to 1922; the president of the Italian Academy; the president of the Fascist Institute of Culture; the president of Balilla; the president of the Fascist Confederations of Laborers; one of the presidents of the Confederations of Employers; the president of the National Society of Co-operatives; and the president of the Special Tribunal for the Defense of the State. In addition the president of the Grand Council may ask others to participate "who have given ample proof of their devotion to Fascism and of their eager willingness to work." The Grand Council convenes at the call of the president.

Until December, 1928, this body was merely an organ of the Fascist party, but then it was given a legal position in the machinery of the state.[5] On the recommendation of the head of the government, the Grand Council appoints the general secretary of the party, the assistant secretaries, and the other members of the Directorate of the party. Prior to 1928 no public provision had been made for Mussolini's successor, but since the law was passed which gave the Grand Council an official place in the state, this body has been required to keep in readiness a list of persons so that in case of the death of Il Duce the Crown will know whom to name in his place.

The Directorate consists of eight members of the Grand Council besides the general secretary and a general administrative secretary. The Directorate is called together once a month by the Duce and whenever the general secretary chooses.

The general secretary determines the procedure of the Directorate and of the various departments and appoints the personnel. The administrative secretary is in charge of the finances of the party, prepares a budget and financial report for the examination and approval of the Directorate, and is responsible for running the various offices of the party.

The departments into which the party organization is divided are the following:

(1) The Political Secretariat: It has charge of all the local party officers and sees to it "that every activity

[5] See p. 146.

of the Party conforms with the Spirit of Fascism." In addition it controls the following organizations:

a) Association of Fascist Teachers.

b) Association of Fascist Railroad Workers.

c) Association of Fascist Postal, Telegraph, and Telephone Employees.

Finally it must keep in touch with and co-operate with:

a) The commander-in-chief of the militia.

b) The general secretary of *fasci* in foreign countries.

c) The presidents of the various confederations of syndicates.

d) The president of the National Association of Co-operatives.

(2) The Administrative Secretariat (headed by the administrative secretary).

(3) Enti Autarchici (various independent national associations).

(4) The press.

(5) Propaganda.

(6) Juvenile organizations.

(7) Feminine *fasci*.

(8) Associations of the Families of Fallen Fascists.

(9) Associations of University Students.

(10) Sport and Dopolavoro (National Association for Physical Education).

(11) Syndicates and co-operatives.

This is an outline of the *national* organization and scope of the Fascist party. The *local* organization consists of (1) the provincial federations of *Fasci,* and (2) the local *Fasci*.

(1) The provincial federations of *fasci:* Each provincial federation is headed by a provincial secretary, ap-

pointed by the general secretary of the party. (Italy has ninety-two provinces.)

The provincial secretaries, when called together by the National Directorate, constitute the National Council. This Council meets to "examine the activities of the Party and receive general executive orders," but it has no power.

The provincial secretary selects seven associates from the Fascists of the province and these, when ratified by the general secretary, constitute the Provincial Directorate. It must meet at least once a month. One of the members serves as provincial administrative secretary. He has charge of the finances and his accounts and reports are examined by a national board of auditors.

The provincial secretary, with the assistance of the directorate, is charged with:

a) Promoting the party's activities in the province and executing the orders of the National Directorate.

b) Supervising the following organizations: (1) Federation of Enti Autarchici; (2) the party press; (3) juvenile organizations; (4) feminine *fasci;* (5) the various "cultural, economic, and athletic" activities of the province.

c) Co-operating with: (1) Fascist senators and deputies; (2) provincial commander of the militia; (3) organizations of syndicates; (4) co-operative organizations; (5) associations under the direction of the party.

d) Appointing and convening (every six months) the secretaries of the local *fasci* of his province.

e) Acting as secretary of the *fascio* of the capital city of his province.

(2) The local *fasci:* These are headed by secretaries appointed by the provincial secretary. The local secretary in turn selects five members of his *fascio,* who, when

ratified by the provincial secretary, constitute the directorate of the *fascio*. One of these members is appointed administrative secretary. The local directorate fixes the dues, but 2 lire for each member must go to the provincial and national offices of the party. The local expenditures must be carefully accounted and submitted annually to the auditing board and provincial administrative secretary.

The articles governing the activities of the local *fascio* are given in full. (They constitute Article 25–33 and *norme generali* of the Constitution.)

The *fascio* is the fundamental organism in the life of the Party and should gather around its standard those Italians who are most reliable for intelligence, honesty, and courage. Since, on the one hand, all moral, economic, and social activities are regulated by the action of the *fascio,* and since, on the other hand, every disturbance and every conflict in the life of the *fascio* is re-echoed in all the other social organisms, every member of the rank and file should feel the weight of this responsibility individually.

The Secretary of a *fascio* will convene an assembly of all Fascists at the beginning of each year to communicate and explain the program which he intends to follow. The widest freedom of discussion must be allowed to all Fascists. During the year, on whatever date seems most opportune, at least one more assembly must be held.

Membership cards will be distributed at the headquarters of each *fascio* with solemn ceremonies on the 23rd of March, the anniversary of the founding of the *fasci di combattimento*. New members will take the following oath before the Secretary: "I swear to obey the orders of the Duce without question and to serve the cause of the Fascist Revolution with all my strength and, if necessary, with my blood."

Every secretary of a *fascio* must know the moral qualifications of every member, as well as his means of livelihood.

Whenever a Fascist falls short of his duty by breach of discipline or by deficiency in those qualities which constitute the Fascist spirit—Faith, Courage, Industry, and Honesty—he must be subjected to an inquiry by the Directorate.

The disciplinary punishments are: (1) deploring the faults, (2) suspension for a definite or indefinite period, (3) expulsion.

No punishment may be inflicted before the guilt of the person has been ascertained and he has been given an opportunity to defend himself.

Every punishment must be reported to the superior officers up to the General Secretary, and is not official until ratified.

A Fascist expelled from the ranks of the Party is a traitor to the Cause and must be banished from political life. No *fascio* can be dissolved without authorization by the General Secretary of the Party.

No Fascist who has not been a member of the Party for at least two years can hold provincial offices.

No provincial director can take on or hold remunerative offices in public bodies, institutions affiliated with the state or economic bodies dependent on local administrations.

Every Fascist, even in the conduct of his professional duties, must bring his work into conformity with the spirit and discipline of Fascism.

4. *The party as a civic educator.*—The highly centralized organization of the party effected by this Constitution and the spirit of discipline which it breathes are, of course, Fascist ideals and not realized facts. Ever since Turati took office, however, he has been actively engaged in the work of centralization and "purification." One *fascio* after another, one province after another, is inspected by him. Wherever he finds local disturbances, personal rivalries, factions, or insubordinations he makes whatever changes of personnel may be necessary. Some of the outlying provinces naturally have caused most trouble, as for example, Palermo (Sicily), Trento, Trieste, Teramo; but some of the oldest centers of Fascism and Fascist violence have also been troublesome to the National party because of their local ambitions and factions, as, for example, Spezia, Piacenza, and Pisa.

More serious than this political problem, however, is the moral discipline of the *fasci*. During the year 1926, 30,000 Fascists were expelled. Almost every issue of the *Foglio d'Ordini,* the official gazette of the party, contains

a list of expulsions, and occasionally one sees in it reports
like the following:

> The General Secretary has expelled from the Party Bernardo
> Palombieri, Assistant Federal Secretary of Teramo, because he has
> given clear evidence of disloyalty towards his own Federal Secretary,
> showing an absolute inability to carry on the work of a director and
> setting his own selfish vanity before the higher interests of the Party.[6]

On the other hand, that there is a tendency on the part
of provincial officers to abuse expulsion is evident from
the following announcement of Secretary Turati:

> The General Secretary of the Party has already earnestly called
> the attention of the Provincial officers of the Party to the *excessive*
> ease with which they resort to the serious measure of expulsion. . . . .
> For every Fascist who is really a soldier in the service of the Idea
> and bound by an oath, public reproof or suspension are in themselves
> very serious measures. . . . . Only when the person's misdeed is
> repeated and his indiscipline takes on the form of rebellion against
> his superiors, or when there are reasons involving his moral character
> (well established, however), is it necessary to resort to expulsion. In
> any case, the inquiry into his guilt and faults must be made with great
> care and strictness and the motivation must be known precisely and in
> detail.[7]

That there is a great deal of restiveness within the
ranks is readily imaginable. The political and military
emergency is over, squadrism and reprisals are prohibited, and "politics" is restricted to the few. It is therefore
not easy to find serious work for the *fasci*. The tendency
is to indulge in parades, banquets, and celebrations of all
sorts. The party has attempted to interfere by prohibiting the wholesale erection of monuments to the "martyrs," the distribution of medals and honors, and all
forms of luxurious celebration. Provincial secretaries are
not allowed to take summer vacations. Three national
Fascist holidays have been established: March 23 (anni-

[6] From *Foglio d'Ordini*, December 24, 1927.

[7] From *Foglio d'Ordini*, October 3, 1927.

versary of the founding of *fasci,* celebrated by the *Leva Fascista,* the initiation of new members in the militia) ; April 21 ("birthday of Rome," labor day, celebrated by the syndicates) ; October 28 (anniversary of the March on Rome, beginning of the Fascist year, celebrated by military parades and convocations). Apart from these holidays, celebrations are (at least officially) discouraged. Even speech-making is frowned upon. The forms of activity which are officially encouraged are: (1) military drill and marches; (2) sport and various forms of organized athletics; (3) supervision of patriotic education among the juvenile organizations (Balilla, Avanguardia, etc.) ; (4) undertaking useful public works (aqueducts, roads, houses, etc.) ; (5) professional training for political careers.

Early Fascism and squadrism was naturally inclined to be licentious, and therefore the party is making strenuous efforts at reform and is trying to build up a puritanic morale and strict discipline in the interests of moral education as well as of politics. The chief appeals, however, which are made to the members of the party in urging this puritanic, military discipline are:

(1) The economic necessities of the people: Italy is continually pictured as waging economic battles, "the battle of the *lira,*" the "battle of grain," "the proletarian struggle against the plutocratic nations," and so on.

(2) The tradition of heroic suffering, which is the cornerstone of Italian patriotism: The heroes of the *risorgimento,* especially Garibaldi, are continually exalted in speeches, movies, textbooks, and so forth. The present hardships, both economic and political, are represented as a natural continuation of Italy's heroic tragic life.

(3) The aspiration toward empire and toward *la*

grandezza del popolo italiano: The serious business and tremendous obligation of building the "New Italy" is impressed on the Fascist imagination.

That the Fascist party is tending rapidly to become, in the main, an association of young people's patriotic societies, is brought out by the following statistics in Table V:[8]

TABLE V

Members in:	1925	1926	1927
Fasci di combattimento	700,000	780,000	813,000
Feminine fasci	25,000	43,000	66,000
Giovani Italiane (adolescent girls)		12,000	50,000
Piccole Italiane (young girls)		75,000	238,000
University groups		9,000	13,000
Advance Guard (adolescent boys)	90,000	180,000	430,000
Balilla (young boys)	70,000	250,000	590,000

It will be seen at once that most of the growth is in the juvenile organizations.

Early in 1927 the doors of the party were definitely closed to all except graduates from the Advance Guard. Within a year or so after the march on Rome, 250,000 persons had joined the party without belonging to the militia. Mussolini, in response to the "Old Guard" propaganda and in order to keep Fascism from changing its political complexion entirely, expelled 150,000 of these. And since then the "purifications" have fallen heavily on those who were not active in the militia. As a result the party is tending more and more to become a militant, patriotic organization of young men and women, and consequently its activities are becoming increasingly "cultural" and social, rather than strictly political.

[8] These figures are taken from the reports given out by Secretary Turati, but they vary so considerably from month to month that only an approximation is possible.

5. *The rôle of the party in the latest constitutional reforms.*—Two recent events, however, of prime importance have reinforced the political status of the party.

(1) The parliamentary reform, passed in March, 1928: This reform provides that a list of about 800 candidates for the Chamber of Deputies be drawn up by the thirteen confederations; that this list be submitted to the Grand Council of the Fascist party, which (*a*) examines the political qualifications of the candidates and rejects any who are not of "reliable Fascist faith," (*b*) adds candidates of its own, (*c*) draws up a final list of 400 candidates to be presented as a whole to the voters, that is, to the members of syndicates, for ratification or rejection *en bloc.*

The first practical application of this scheme was made in the spring of 1929, following the dissolution of the old Chamber, December 8, 1928. The confederations drew up their list of 800, and the Grand Council reduced this number to 400, of whom 191 had been members of the old Chamber. Of the 400 candidates, 82 represented the National Federation of Syndicates of Intellectuals; 46, the Confederation of Agriculturalists; 40, the National Association of Veterans; 31, the Confederation of Industry; 27, the Syndicates of Agricultural Laborers; 26, the Syndicates of Industrial Workers; 16, the Confederation of Merchants; 15, the universities; 14, the National Association of War Cripples and Invalids; 12, the Confederation of Land Transportation and Inland Navigation; 11, the Syndicates of Seamen and Airmen; 10, the Syndicates of Merchants and National Institute of Co-operatives; 10, the Confederation of Bankers; 10, the Confederation of Maritime and Aerial Transportation, and the remainder, other small groups. This list was submitted to an electorate of about nine and a half million voters, and was accepted by a vote of 8,514,000 to 136,000, March 24.[9] Obviously this gives the party complete control over the Chamber of Deputies.

While this important change was being effected, the Fascists were planning to extend their sway over the Senate. This was comparatively easy, for it necessitated only the appointment of a sufficient number of Fascists to insure a safe majority. The new senators were named at various times during the winter of 1928–29, and now Italy's Upper House is under Fascist control.

(2) The Fascist party has still further fortified its position by making its Grand Council an official organ of the state:[10] This body has become the "supreme organ, co-ordinating all the activities of the Régime. . . . ." Among its duties are the deliberation in a consultative fashion on all matters submitted to it by the government, the selection of the candidates for the Chamber, the selection of the successor to Mussolini, approval of all bills of a constitutional nature,[11] the approval of the successor to the throne, and the administration of the Fascist party. The importance of this law is not difficult to estimate. It means that the Grand Council, and with it the Fascist party, is the highest body in the state. It can dictate all the policies which are to be applied by the leaders of all the "forces" in the nation, and progress in their applica-

[9] In this first election held under the reformed system suffrage was not limited to members of syndicates, but was extended to include also those who paid a direct tax of at least 100 lire, those who held state bonds to the value of 500 lire or more, or who received an official pension or salary, and members of the clergy or ministers of any cult recognized by the state. The vote was extended to men only. The age limit was established at twenty-one, but men eighteen years old who were married and fathers of children were allowed to exercise the right of suffrage.

[10] Law of December 10, 1928.

[11] Constitutional laws are defined by the law which made the Grand Council an official body, Art. 12.

tion is to be reported by Il Duce every five years in a monumental reunion of all the chiefs in Rome.[12]

Protests against these changes have not been wanting. The veteran Giolitti raised his voice in opposition, but he was politely ignored and the *Foglio d'Ordini* bluntly announced: "The Constitution *(Statuto)* was made in 1848; now we are living in 1928." Nevertheless it should be added that these reforms have been realized with formal legality, for the *Statuto* of 1848 provided that it could be amended by simple parliamentary legislation. Though the changes were made gradually within the legal forms of the Constitution, the spirit of the Italian government has been completely revolutionized. The transformation of the Grand Council of the Fascist party into the chief organ of the government has "inserted the Party into the State." It has definitely put an end to "the dualism between Party and State," and thereby has put an end to the last vestiges of party politics and parliamentary government.

[12] The first meeting of this sort was held March 10, 1929.

CHAPTER IX
THE FASCIST PRESS

1. *Fascism essentially journalistic.*—At the present time it would be useless to describe the importance of the press in forming public opinion. Everyone recognizes that since the middle of the nineteenth century cheap and widely circulating newspapers have been the most effective weapons in waging battles of political thought among the common people. The Fascists have been aware of this fact, and in their experiment journalism and journalists have played important rôles. Scores of Fascist leaders are ex-journalists and many of them still have their own papers as mouthpieces for individual expression. The party itself finds the press one of its chief mainstays and uses many papers as its official or semiofficial supporters.

Mussolini, himself a journalist, declared at the Congress of the National Fascist Syndicate of Journalists held at Rome, January 28, 1924:

> Certainly among all those things which may be called prodigious in our civilization journalism (perhaps too mechanical) holds first place. The newspaper is the mirror of the world. In the press one looks down on the great street of the world and sees everything which has to do with the human race—everything from high politics to simple events.

And on another occasion Mussolini said: "Journalism is the daily parliament, the daily platform where men from universities, from the sciences, from the industries and from daily life thresh out problems with a competence seldom found on the benches of Parliament."[1]

[1] Speech to the Senate, July 8, 1923.

2. *Fascist policy in controlling public opinion.*—How
the news is interpreted is of vital importance to every political régime, and for Fascism this interpretation constitutes a "mission of the highest responsibility."[2] Prefects
frequently order the suppression of news items,[3] and the
Fascist party has ordered a strict censorship of all printed matter concerning Fascism.[4]

It is difficult to describe the policy followed by Fascism in controlling public opinion through the press, but
in general the following is true:

(1) Events, which the party desires to hush up, are
entirely excluded from the news—for example, deeds of
violence by Fascists, reprisals taken, activities of the em-
igré opposition: Occasionally a general reference is made
to "local disturbances," "sporadic indiscipline," "slander-
ous accusations," or something of the sort, but never anything specific.

(2) Issues which arise within the party or government, debates and discussions reflecting various points of
view or conflicting interests, are announced only in terms
of the final action taken: No direct indication is given of
the motives, occasions and causes of a decree, a reform, a
resolution by the Council or any official action. Usually
the final decision is labeled the "will of the Duce," and the
impression is given that everything is Mussolini's personal handiwork.

(3) An account of Fascist activities is supplemented
by a liberal amount of praise, the insertion of laudatory
adjectives and a flow of patriotic rhetoric.

(4) Editorial comments and articles are expository

[2] *Ibid.*

[3] See, for instance, the article, "La Stampa e Gli Uffici Competenti," in
L'Impero, of Rome, July 5, 1928.

[4] Circulars of the party of January 21 and September 29, 1927, and of
April 5, 1928.

and laudatory, not critical: However, the art of reading between the lines is soon acquired, and intelligent readers of the papers, accustomed to the implications of certain apparently innocent phrases and formulas, can get more information than appears on the surface. Frequently, for example, a patriotic prologue and an epilogue in praise of the Duce are used to conceal critical remarks. Such remarks are always couched in cautious terms and made to appear as humble opinions of a friendly observer, and if possible some remark or action of Mussolini's is used as a pretext or shelter. To appear an ardent disciple of Mussolini personally even while criticizing Fascist policies is an old game by this time.

3. *Fascist legislation on the press.*—The Italian Constitution of 1848 stated that "the Press is free" but "future laws will prevent its abuse."[5] Various governments have had different conceptions of the "abuse" of the press; some have been very lenient and some very severe. The Fascist government may be classed among the latter. It has rigorously enforced the press laws which it found in effect in 1922, and has attempted by new legislation to enlist the press in the Fascist army of propagandists. It has enforced a law which requires an editor to give the state three copies of every published work. One copy is deposited in the Central National Library at Florence, another in the Victor Emmanuel Library at Rome (except juridical works, which are placed in the Library of the Ministry of Justice), and the third in the university or governmental library of the province in which the work is published.

The Fascist government has retained laws which demand that everyone who wishes to open a printing establishment must obtain the permission of the police author-

[5] Art. 28.

ities,[6] and that everyone who wishes to found a newspaper or other periodical must make a declaration to the Ministry of the Interior giving detailed information concerning the project.[7] It demands that every newspaper have a legally responsible editor *(gerente)*.[8] The editor named must not be a nonentity or a person immune from prosecution (deputy or senator), as was possible and common before Fascism, but the actual director or one of the leading editors. His appointment must be approved by the attorney general of the province and every application for appointment as responsible editor must be accompanied by a full report concerning the periodical. The state has rights to the property of any periodical in default of fines.[9] Papers may no longer publish what they please and let the blame fall on some obscure person. Under the new system it is a serious matter in the life of a journal if its *gerente* is found guilty of breaking the press laws.

Besides this attempt to fix responsibility for periodicals on important people the Fascist Régime has made laws to control the news. Prefects have been given power to summon and to take action against the responsible editors in the following cases:

(1) If a newspaper or periodical by means of false or misleading news complicates the diplomatic action of the Government in its relation with foreign countries, or depreciates the national credit at home or abroad, or unjustly alarms the populace, or in any way disturbs the public peace;

[6] Decree of June 30, 1889.

[7] Art. 36, Law of March 26, 1848.

[8] Art. 37, Law of March 26, 1848. See also Ermanno Amicucci, "Il Giornalismo nel Regime Fascista," in *La Civiltà Fascista* (Turin: U.T.E.T., 1928), pp. 495–98.

[9] Royal Decree of July 15, 1923, converted into the Law of December 31, 1925, Arts. 5 and 6.

(2) If a newspaper . . . . excites crime or class hatred or diso-
bedience of the laws and orders of public authorities, or disturbs the
discipline of employees in a public service, or favors the interests of
foreign states, associations, or individuals to the detriment of Italian
interests, or disparages the Fatherland, the King, the Royal family,
the Pope, the religion, institutions, and powers of the State and of
friendly powers.[10]

4. *Fascist organization of the journalist profession.*
—As a further guaranty against attacks from the press
an effort has been made to control the personnel of the
journalist profession. A Professional Roll of Journalists has been created and no one may practice the profession whose name does not appear on this list.[11] In this
way professional journalists, apprentices, and publicists
are minutely controlled. Every applicant for admission
to the Roll must give ample proof of good moral and political standing, the latter being judged not only by the
officials in charge of the Roll, but also by the prefect of
the province.[12] Foreigners may practice the profession of
journalism provided they fulfil the same requirements.[13]

In addition to these political checks on the personnel
of the profession an attempt has been made to improve
the quality of journalism. To this end courses in journalism have been founded in many of the universities, usually in the faculties of political science, and since June 30,
1928, a secondary school diploma or its equivalent is required for admission to the Professional Roll.[14]

The most important organization of newspapermen
is the National Fascist Syndicate of Journalists, which
is affiliated with the National Federation of Fascist In-

[10] Decree of July 15, 1923, converted into the Law of December 31, 1925,
No. 2309, Art. 2.

[11] Decree of February 20, 1928, Art. 1.

[12] *Ibid.,* Arts. 5 and 6.

[13] *Ibid.,* Art. 7.   [14] Decree of February 20, 1928, Art. 16.

tellectual Syndicates and thus automatically with the National Confederation of Fascist Syndicates.[15] The National Fascist Syndicate of Journalists has its headquarters in Rome and is managed by a general secretary and a directorate, whose members are appointed by the eleven regional syndicates. It publishes the *Bollettino* (bimonthly) and the *Annuario della Stampa Italiana*. Its purpose is to secure work for its members, to make known and defend the rights of journalists, to settle labor disputes for them, to insure the application of laws on labor and social insurance, and to diffuse among its members general technical culture by means of lectures and publications.[16] The syndicate keeps the Professional Roll, and is thus able to admit or dismiss men from the profession. The Syndicate of Journalists has bargained with the Syndicate of Employers of Journalists (the National Fascist Association of Newspaper Editors)[17] and secured a contract which is very favorable to newspapermen.[18] The syndicate has founded a National Institute for the Insurance of Italian Journalists which, under the direction of Mussolini's brother, Arnaldo, is apparently a great success. In connection with these reforms the new law on the rights of authors should be mentioned. Although it was passed before the syndicate was created, it has the syndicate's approval, for it greatly improved the conditions under which writers may market their works.

5. *The non-partisan press.*—Fascism tolerates no opposition on the part of the newspapers, and when it has failed to convert, reorganize, or buy opposition sheets it

[15] *Statuto del Sindacato Nazionale Fascista dei Giornalisti*, Arts. 1 to 4.

[16] *Ibid.*, Art. 7.

[17] Founded in 1922 but reorganized in 1926. Headquarters: Via Ciovasso 4, Milan.

[18] Text of the contract may be found in the *Annuario della Stampa Italiana* (1927–28), pp. 101 ff.

has employed more direct means of action. There still exists, however, an important group of old established papers which have been forced to assent to Fascism but are in no sense organs of the party. Foremost among these are: *Il Corriere della Sera,* of Milan, formerly the most distinguished Liberal paper in Italy and still one of the most widely circulated; *La Stampa,* of Turin, also of Liberal traditions and the second largest Italian paper; *Il Giornale d'Italia,* of Rome. These dignified, conservative (i.e., Liberal) papers have survived the revolution, but have lost much of their traditional excellence and prestige. Most of the old editors hae been forced out and the distinguished contributors hushed up. Among the other important old papers that have survived, the following should be mentioned: *La Nazione,* of Florence, which dates from 1858 and enjoys considerable prestige in Tuscany; *Il Mezzogiorno,* of Naples, founded in 1818; *Il Messagero,* of Rome (1878); the *Gazetta Di Venezia* (1742), and *Il Resto del Carlino,* of Bologna.

The Agenzia Stefani, a press agency similar to the Associated Press in America and Havas in France, is still intact and furnishes national and international news to any newspaper which cannot afford a large staff of private correspondents. This agency ranks among the largest four in the world, and the Fascists were not slow in realizing the importance of securing its co-operation. By means of this agency it is obviously easy to supply uniform, censored, and officially approved political news to all Italian papers. Official announcements and news favorable to Fascism are continually issued by Stefani both at home and abroad.

In the strict sense of the word, there is, of course, no opposition press. Only *L'Osservatore Romano,* the political organ of the Vatican, still remains free to criticize the new order openly, but it seldom goes further than to discuss those policies which directly concern the church, and to publish without comment news items which are suppressed in other papers.

The Italian press has learned by bitter experience or observation that whereas technical criticism will be tolerated and even welcomed, opposition is impossible. In 1925 the Socialist papers *Unita, Giustizia,* and *Avanti,* and the Republican *Voce Repubblicana,* and the Liberal *Il Mondo* were suppressed outright. Even the *Corriere della Sera* and the *Giornale d'Italia* were suspended for short periods. The *Secolo,* of Milan, was bought from ardent opponents of Fascism and reorganized with a new and less combative program. In 1926 *La Stampa,* of Turin, was suppressed for a time along with several others, most of which have since been revived and have refrained from further opposition, having learned their lessons. A leading humorous and satirical sheet, *Il Becco Giallo* (The Yellow Beak), was persecuted when it began satirizing Fascism; for a while its cover appeared with a padlock on the beak, but then the editor was further intimidated until he went out of business entirely.

6. *Fascist newspapers.*—The most Fascist of all newspapers—those sheets which come the nearest to being official organs of Fascism—are *Il Popolo d'Italia,* of Milan, and *La Tribuna,* of Rome. The former was founded by Benito Mussolini in 1914 but since November, 1922, has been directed by his brother, Arnaldo. *Il Popolo* mirrors more perfectly than any other sheet the ideas of Fascism's leader. It is ever ready to take up the cudgel against those Socialist doctrines which it once sponsored, to defend Fascism in questions of church and state, to glorify Italy at the expense of other nations, to denounce attacks on Fascism in violent terms, and to sing the

praises of the new order. Its influence is greater than that
of any other Fascist paper; it enjoys a very wide circulation, and its articles and editorials are cited and commented upon in many leading newspapers. It is still
looked upon as voicing the personal opinions of the Duce,
though he now takes little active part in its direction and
occasionally even contradicts opinions and policies expressed in it. *La Tribuna* was formerly *L'Idee Nazionale* (founded in 1883)—the organ of the Nationalist party—and now is an outstanding mouthpiece of Fascism.
It, too, paints the Régime in the brightest colors, and is
always ready to display a bristled front on international matters. Its director is Roberto Forges-Davanzati.
Whereas the *Popolo d'Italia* is chiefly interested in internal affairs, the *Tribuna,* being still under Nationalist
influence, features foreign policy. On syndicalist and
economic issues it is usually more conservative than the
Popolo d'Italia.

In almost the same category as these two papers, but
less apt to reflect correctly the Fascism of Mussolini, are
the following: *Il Lavoro d'Italia,* of Rome, the widely
circulated organ of Fascist syndicalism, founded in 1926
and directed by Edmondo Rossoni; *L'Impero,* of Rome,
founded in 1923, a jingoist daily which represents the imperialist, "intransigent," and futurist elements of Fascism, and whose chief editors and contributors are Mario
Carli, Emilio Settimelli, and F. T. Marinetti; *Il Regime
Fascista* (formerly *Cremona Nuova*), one of the pio-
neers of Fascism, founded in 1922, and directed by Roberto Farinacci (its violence and "intransigence" is only
rivaled by that of *L'Impero*), and *Il Tevere* (1924), of
Rome, a Fascist daily directed by Telesio Interlandi.

In a class by itself is the *Foglio d'Ordini,* the official
sheet of the Fascist party. It appears at irregular inter-

vals and is sent to every *fascio* as well as to all officials and organizations affiliated with the party. It is usually four pages long and contains:

(1) Messages from Mussolini: These come usually on the occasion of some celebration.

(2) Official editorials on important events: No news account of the event is given, but merely the official party attitude toward it. If not written by Mussolini, these editorials are usually quite directly inspired by him.

(3) Instructions to party members and orders to the militia.

(4) Notices of disciplinary and punitive measures in the party: Usually there is a considerable list of names under the heading *epurazione e selezione*.   .

(5) Party news, such as promotions, statistics, activities of various *fasci,* etc.

There is one more class of Fascist newspapers—the polemical and "ardent" weeklies. These are usually journalistic efforts of some *fascio* full of fiery propaganda or they are personal organs of some ambitious Fascist journalists. They spring up like mushrooms and many of the more irresponsible ones have been suppressed. Among the best of these sheets are *La Conquista dello Stato,* directed by Curzio Suckert (Malaparte), *Il Selvaggio* and *L'Italiano,* by Ardengo Soffici. Their articles and polemics in defense of Fascism were especially influential during the dissidence movement and "integralist" and "Vocist" Fascists rallied around their banners. At Rome two other papers of much the same sort have had some influence: *Patria,* directed by Renato Manzini, and *Roma Fascista,* edited by Umberto Guglielmotti. In almost all the provincial cities newspapers of a similar nature may be found, *L'Assalto,* edited by Giorgio Pini at Bologna; *Il Nazionale,* by Pietro Gorgolini at Turin; *Battaglie*

Fasciste, at Florence; *Lo Stato,* of Naples, edited by
Bruno Spampanato; and others.

7. *Fascism and periodical literature.*—Fascism has
about the same hold on magazines as on newspapers.
Scores of new reviews have been born of Fascism. In
fact, few of those which are published today (except
scientific periodicals) antedate the Fascist Revolution.
These reviews may be grouped into these three main
classes: political reviews, whose purpose is to propagate
Fascist doctrines; semi-scientific reviews, and literary,
artistic, and popular reviews.

One of the most important reviews of the first group
is *Gerarchia,* a monthly founded by Mussolini in 1921 at
Milan, and now directed by his former colleague and bi-
ographer, Margherita Sarfatti. *Gerarchia* publishes articles by important men on political events and Fascist
doctrines. Of much the same nature is the biweekly *Critica Fascista* (1922) directed by G. Bottai, minister of
corporations. More pretentious, dignified, and scholarly
is the Nationalist bimonthly *Politica.* It was founded
after the war by Francesco Coppola and Alfredo Rocco
in order to revive a vigorous foreign policy in Italy. Most
of the articles of *Politica* reflect the opinions of the Nationalist group, but it has many other distinguished contributors. Magazines like *Rassegna Italiana* and news
reviews like *L'Illustrazione* carry a large amount of nationalist propaganda.

Among the semiscientific periodicals are to be found
those reviews which popularize the doctrines of Fascism.
For instance, there are three periodicals devoted to syndicalism and the corporate state. *Il Diritto del Lavoro*
(1927), whose director is Giuseppe Bottai, is an official
organ of the Ministry of Corporations, and publishes articles of a juridical nature concerning syndicalism. *Lo*

Stato Corporativo (1926) is directed by C. Costamagna, one of the leading legal authorities on Italian syndicalism. *La Stirpe* (1923), whose director is Rossoni, publishes syndicalist information of especial interest to workers and at the same time carries general popular articles.

Of a less technical nature are *Educazione Fascista* (1925, formerly *Educazione Politica*), *Leonardo,* and *Nuovi Studi di Diritto, Economia, e Politica* (1927), published by the idealist and Liberal wing of the party under the direction of Giovanni Gentile, Ugo Spirito, and Luigi Russo, respectively. These reviews carry articles on the philosophy and history of Fascism. *Educazione* is the official organ of the Istituto Nazionale Fascista di Cultura. This institute is headed by Gentile and dominated by his philosophy and educational theory. It publishes high-class propaganda and is the chief center of Fascist intellectuals.[19] *La Vita Nova* (1925), published by the Fascist University of Bologna (a propagandist organization), is directed by Giuseppe Saitta. It has a similar intellectual complexion, but it is more academic and less mature. It is primarily a student sheet.

Among artistic reviews may be mentioned *Pinacoteca,* formerly *Vita Artistica* (1926), and *Augustea* (1925) ; and among literary reviews, the weekly *La Fiera Letteraria* (1925) and *Il 900* (1926), all of which have Fascist directors. Fascist artists and writers receive large praise in these reviews, but on the whole they are less "Fascist" than the political publications.

Almanacs, like that of the *Popolo d'Italia,* are another effective form of propaganda, for by a judicious selection and interpretation of the events of the year they can make current history look like the biography of Mussolini and the calendar like a record of Fascist victories.

[19] See chap. v.

Of the numerous pamphlets, posters, pictures, wall inscriptions, and similar forms of propaganda no detailed
discussion is possible. It may be well, however, to remark
that wall-posters are an old and very prevalent form of
publicity in Italy. Patriotic posters are usually in red,
white, and green; they are posted on prominent buildings
all over Italy, and are usually vibrant with emotional appeal. They are especially important in small villages and
illiterate districts, where the newspaper does not reach
the masses. Extraordinary events, special celebrations,
and official orders are usually made public in this way.
The Fascists have indulged in them freely from the very
start.

8. *Fascist book publication—the Libreria del Littorio.*—Fascism is explained, defended, and propagated
not only in its many periodicals but also in a vast number
of books every year. Almost all important Italian publishing houses have at one time or another printed books
on Fascism, but there are some houses that are much
more important in this respect than others. The outstanding one is La Libreria del Littorio, founded by the Fascist party in 1927 as the center of "Fascist culture in its
various forms and most diverse fields to satisfy amply the
ardent desire of Italians and foreigners to follow the development of Fascist thought. . . . ." It is under the
direct control of the party. Its president is Augusto Turati, secretary of the Fascist party, and its technical council of direction is composed of the presidents of the seven
national confederations, presided over by Mussolini himself. A great many books have already been published by
the Libreria, such as editions of Mussolini's and Turati's
speeches, popular treatises (in the *Collezione Littoria*)
on the various phases of Fascist reforms—finance, economy, and education, and the *Annali del Regime,* a his-

tory of Fascism. In general these books are popular
works of propaganda printed with elaborate Fascist em-
bellishment; there are few scholarly, critical works among
them. The Libreria publishes several periodicals, among
which the most important are the *Foglio d'Ordini,* official organ of the party;[20] the monthly *Bibliografia Fascista,* a supplement to the *Guida Bibliografica del Fascismo,* published by the Libreria in 1928; *Turismo d'Italia,*
a luxurious travel magazine, and a projected *Annuario
dell'Italia Fascista,* whose 2,000 pages will give a complete cross-section of Fascist Italy every year. (The first
number was planned for 1928.) Furthermore, the Libreria del Littorio provides all the services of a high-class
bookstore; its elegant building in the center of Rome and
its branch at Milan are admirably equipped to furnish all
materials published concerning Fascism.

The Libreria del Littorio is the only publishing house
under the direct control of the party. Yet there are others
devoted almost exclusively to the publication of Fascist
books. Of these La Voce is perhaps the most important.
This Fascist Voce publishing house is the successor of
Prezzolini's periodical *La Voce,* and still reflects many of
the political and literary characteristics of the Voce movement. Its director is Curzio Suckert, editor of *La Conquista dello Stato,* and Bottai (as president) and the
Nationalists Coppola and Forges-Davanzati are among
others on its board of administration. La Voce publishes
several periodicals: *La Conquista dello Stato, Politica,*
and *Pinacoteca;* but it has also edited a number of the
more serious books on Fascism, such as the series *I Prob-
lemi del Fascismo* (by Massimo Rocca, Soffici, Bolzon,
Suckert, and others) ; *La Trasformazione dello Stato* (by
A. Rocco) ; *Europa Vivente, Italia Barbara,* and *Don*

[20] See above.

Camalio (by Curzio Suckert), and *Storia di un Camaleonte di Mussolini.* Others less important and yet outstanding editors of Fascist books are: Alpes (formerly Imperia), the publisher of Mussolini's speeches and numerous pieces of propaganda; Bemporad, an old Florentine house, and a prolific producer of all sorts of Fascist literature, and Capelli, of Bologna, editor of many of the earliest Fascist books.

9. *Fascist use of motion pictures.*—Pursuing its policy of enlisting the support of all the agencies which are influential in shaping the ideas of the masses, Fascism has attempted to control to some extent the production, distribution, and showing of motion pictures. The importance of this means of propaganda is evident. There are in Italy 3,256 motion-picture houses, with an average daily attendance of 2,500,000 people.[21] The motion-picture industry offered Fascism an opportunity which could not be missed. Foreign companies had for years furnished the bulk of the films which were shown, for there were no important domestic producers. In 1924 a private corporation was founded for the purpose of producing educational films. This offered Fascism its chance and in September of the same year this company was reorganized as L'Unione Cinematografica Educativa (Luce), all its stock being subscribed by semigovernmental organizations, Commissariato Generale dell'Emigrazione, Cassa Nazionale per le Assicurazioni Sociali, Istituto Nazionale delle Assicurazioni, Opera Nazionale per i Combattenti, and the Cassa Nazionale di Assicurazioni per gli Infortuni degli Operai sul Lavoro. The new organization, "an organ of culture and of Italianization," undertook its task of diffusing "films of a cultural, edu-

[21] *Tre Anni di Vita dell'Istituto Nazionale LUCE,* (Rome: Luce, 1927), p. 57.

cational and scientific nature and those for purposes of
social and national propaganda."[22] To increase the prestige of Luce and to insure state control over it, two decrees were issued declaring the corporation to be the official motion-picture organ of the state, outlining its
duties, regularizing its organization, and bestowing upon
it the more official title of Istituto Nazionale Luce.[23]

The purpose of Luce is to furnish films of an educational and political nature for domestic and foreign consumption. To this end special sections have been created
within the corporation to deal with various categories of
pictures. There is a section to cover pictures related to
each of the following subjects: agriculture, industry
(with branches concerning professional education and
railways), art and religion, national culture, secondary
schools, military instruction and propaganda, travel and
marine propaganda, hygiene, and propaganda abroad.
In addition especial emphasis is placed upon political
propaganda although no separate "section" exists for
this subject. A large number of films have already been
produced. For example, the agricultural section has produced films concerning the culture of grain under the various conditions existing in Italy. The industrial section
has made pictures showing the production of cotton and
silk goods, the construction of locomotives, and the building of hydro-electric plants. The section on art has made
films of the various ruins in Italy—Ostia, the Roman
Forum, Herculaneum, and others. The section on travel
has pictures showing the wonders of Italian scenery, the
magnificence of her new merchant marine, and the construction of a port.

[22] Mussolini in a letter to the various Ministers, October 7, 1925. Repro-
duced in *Tre Anni di Vita dell'Istituto Nazionale Luce*, p. 7.

[23] Decrees of November 5, 1925 and December 24, 1926.

Of especial interest are several political and nationalist films already produced by the section on military education and propaganda, for its purpose is to give technical military instruction and "to show the people the glory won by our Armed Forces in the Great War, documented by the pictures taken during the military operations . . . . to produce war films to compete with foreign war pictures which have found great favor with the public and which have a tendency to depict the valor of the armies of other nations in the World War; and to give in an indirect way advice and suggestions which people may need for the unforeseen events of future wars."[24] Films have been produced showing the use of cannons, the problems of munitions, the rôle of the Italian army during the war (*Guerra Nostra,* which has had a great success), life on board a man-of-war, the militia, etc. In addition to these pictures there is a whole series of a more purely political nature which aims to explain what Fascism is, what it has done, what it is doing, and what it plans to do. The film *Militia* is an attempt not only to popularize militarism but also to impress upon the masses the strength of Fascism by showing them the party's armed force. The colonial problem is treated in *The Return of Rome* and *Our Colonies.* The film *Italia* is devoted to patriotic love of country, and *Vita Nuova* to the renovations which Fascism is making. A number of pictures have been made concerning the activity of the youth organizations, Balilla and Avanguardia, summer camps, military instruction, etc. All conspicuous events, such as Nobile's flights to the North Pole, De Pinedo's flight, the *Leva Fascista,* the visit of the king or princes to various parts of Italy, important celebrations, and athletic

[24] *Tre Anni di Vita dell'Istituto Nazionale Luce,* pp. 36–37.

meets—all these are filmed and distributed while the iron
is still hot. But films of Mussolini catch the popular imagination most of all. Every time he appears in public he
is filmed. One Mussolini picture, *Il Duce,* has already
been released and has been a great triumph both at home
and abroad.

The development of Luce during its short period of
existence has been remarkable. It has established an international weekly news reel, made contracts with the
leading foreign producers, and succeeded in establishing
at Rome the International Institute of Educational Cin-
emas, an organ of the League of Nations. It has received
exceptional support from theater directors and the government. On March 27, 1926, the National Syndicate of
Commercial Films voted that the showing of Luce films
be made obligatory. The government accepted this sug-
gestion and issued a decree to the effect that every motion-picture house show daily one film "of the sort" produced by Luce.[25] The complete enforcement of this law
was at first impossible, but Luce now furnishes films for
about 3,000 Italian theaters every day, a total of over
1,500,000 meters a year. In order that these films might be
shown to the people in towns which do not boast motion-
picture houses, traveling theaters—autobuses equipped
with the necessary machines and an electrical apparatus
—have been established. There are twenty-five of these
cinema *ambulanti* and in the first four months of their existence they had given gratuitously 2,500 programs before from six to seven million people.[26]

Luce has also begun to make its importance felt
abroad. By means of reciprocal agreements with foreign

[25] Decree of April 3, 1926.

[26] *Tre Anni di Vita dell'Istituto Nazionale Luce,* p. 64.

producers Luce films have made their way into every foreign country. Besides those pictures which are exported in the regular commercial way, Luce sends a great many abroad as pure propaganda. In 1926, for instance, 120,-000 meters were sent abroad free of charge. This activity has been especially noticeable in Switzerland, which alone received 2,400 films in 1926. Luce maintains absolutely free of charge one traveling cinema in Albania and another in Cyrenaica.

CHAPTER X

VARIOUS PATRIOTIC ORGANIZATIONS[1]

1. *Fascist youth organizations.*—"Every good Fascist knows that the life of the Party has its *raison d'être* in the old Black Shirts, who serenely faced the cruel struggle in the severest years of the nation's history, and that the Party is not sure of a future unless it can incorporate and organize the recruits of Fascism—unless the arms, hearts and minds of the youth are prepared for new conquests."[2]

In these words Mussolini stated what every Italian believes—that the future of Fascism in the next generation depends largely upon the education of the youth. Firmly convinced of this basic principle, the Régime has created youth organizations with more than a million and a quarter members, and has dissolved all those agencies which might compete with them, for instance, the Catholic Boy Scouts. This measure was taken March 28, 1928. The Fascist reasons for this act were that the organizations of the Régime were purely Italian and sufficient for Italy, that the Boy Scouts were imbued with democratic ideas of government, and that the military instruction given by other than Fascist organizations might be dangerous for the new order. Thus Fascism

[1] Many Italian patriotic societies have been treated in other chapters. Nearly all those of a military nature will be found in chapter vi; those of an imperialistic nature in chapter iii; those of an educational nature in chapter v. In the present chapter those organizations which have not been discussed in connection with other subjects will be described. For a complete list of patriotic societies see the Index, under patriotic societies.

[2] Speech by Mussolini before the Grand Council of the party, February 13, 1925.

has jealously created a monopoly of control over the Italian youth.

Immediately after the march on Rome the party was faced with the problem of organizing the boys and youths who had given what support they could to the movement. The more mature youths were embodied in the militia,[3] adolescent boys were organized to form the Avanguardia, and the youngest became the Balilla.[4] Gradually Avanguardia and Balilla assumed a character of their own. They undertook the task of giving young Italians physical, Fascist, patriotic, and military instruction.

In 1925 Balilla and Avanguardia became integral parts of the Fascist political organization. Two years later admission to the party was closed except by promotion from Avanguardia. The promotion ceremonies take place every year on the anniversary of the founding of the *fasci di combattimento*.[5] The eldest boys in Balilla enter Avanguardia and the eldest in Avanguardia enter the militia and the party. When the boys enter the militia they take this vow: "I swear to obey the orders of the *Duce* without question, and to serve the cause of the Fascist Revolution with all my strength and, if necessary with my blood." And having sworn this oath, each boy receives a rifle as a symbol of his faith and a means of fulfilling his "duty."

This *Leva Fascista* (Fascist levy) is the occasion of great patriotic exuberances. In 1928 Mussolini addressed this message to his followers:

Black Shirts of all Italy!
Today is the ninth anniversary of the creation of the Italian *fasci*

[3] See chap. vi.

[4] Balilla was the nickname of a youthful Genoese, Giovanni Battista Perasso, who was the hero of the campaign against the Austrians at Genoa in 1746.

[5] See *Leva Fascista*, p. 194, in chap. xi.

di combattimento. You will celebrate it with memories and with action. Eighty thousand sons of the Italian people enter the powerful political and military organizations of the Régime.

Avanguardisti!

The veterans of Fascism await you with a perfect spirit of fraternity and with joyful pride. Be proud to receive the badge of the Party and the musket of the Militia. This dual consecration makes you citizens of the Régime and soldiers of the Nation.

Black Shirts!

With every year that passes, the base of the pyramid is larger. The Régime coincides ever more exactly with the boundaries of the Nation. Great numbers of youths are added to other still greater numbers. Millions of men form the armed guarantee of the Fascist Revolution.

Salute with a loud voice the new generation of the Lictor's Rods, with the cry of our vigilant *arditi* and squadrists: *A Noi!*[6]

In 1926 a national law gave Balilla and Avanguardia a legal status.[7] The inclusive National Foundation Balilla for the Physical and Moral Education of the Youth was created. Its component parts are Balilla, for boys from eight to fourteen, and Avanguardia, for those from fourteen to eighteen. Under the stimulus of the new organization the membership of both groups has increased by leaps and bounds. By April 1928, 430,000 were enrolled in Avanguardia and 590,000 in Balilla.[8]

The purpose of the youth organizations is "to train boys both physically and morally that they may be worthy of the new order of Italian life."[9] As a guaranty that Fascist doctrines will be inculcated, the leaders are in almost every case officers of the Fascist militia. Moreover an attempt is made to bring the boys under the romantic spell of Fascism. They are organized in squads, centu-

[6] *Foglio d'Ordini,* March 23, 1928.

[7] Law of April 3.

[8] *Foglio d'Ordini,* April 20, 1928.

[9] Art. 1, Law of April 3, 1926, No. 2247.

ries, and legions, in imitation of the Roman army. Their uniforms consist of black shirts, black fez, and green-gray trousers. They are confronted with masses of Fascist propaganda. They receive the official *Bollettino dell'Opera Nazionale Balilla* and *Il Balilla* of *Il Popolo d'Italia*. They attend lectures and participate in the patriotic enthusiasm created on such occasions as the *Leva Fascista*. A whole flood of books has already been written for them.

In every respect they are made to appear as small editions of adult Fascists. Part of the education which is to make the boys worthy of the new Italy is purely military. They are submitted to rigid military discipline. They must salute all superiors in the Roman fashion; they march in military style, they obey as every soldier must; otherwise they are punished according to martial law. In the Avanguardia serious military instruction is given in preparation for entering the army.[10] That the physical side of their development may not be neglected every local organization has an athletic field, or the use of one, and great emphasis is placed on sports. Competitive track meets between troops and a national meet are held every year. During the summer, camps much on the order of American boys' camps but more military, and cruises on the sea are open to the boys.

Although the party places greatest emphasis on training the boys, it has not neglected the girls. The last few years have witnessed the growth of organizations for girls similar to Balilla and Avanguardia; Piccole Italiane corresponds to the former and Giovani Italiane to the latter. Their purpose is to teach the Italian girl:

1. To fulfil her duties as daughter, sister, student, and friend, with cheerfulness and joy even though they be fatiguing.

[10] See chap. vi.

2. To serve the Nation as her other and greater mother, the mother of all good Italians.

3. To love the *Duce* who has made the Nation stronger and greater.

4. To obey her superiors with joy.

5. To have the courage to repulse those who give evil council and deride honesty.

6. To educate the body to withstand physical fatigue and the spirit not to show pain.

7. To abhor stupid vanity but to love beautiful things.

8. To love work which is life.[11]

In order to attain these ends the methods of Balilla and Avanguardia are used. The girls have uniforms, white blouses, black skirts, white stockings, and black bérets. They are given physical education; they are taken to camps in the summer, and they are taught the elements of Fascism by lectures. To be sure, they do not get the military drill which is given the boys, but that they may get patriotic stimulus from time to time they make pilgrimages to war monuments, are shown patriotic films, and are harangued by nationalist orators.[12] In 1928 there were 49,750 girls in the Giovani Italiane and 238,333 in Piccole Italiane.[13]

2. *Dopolavoro.—Dopolavoro* is not properly speaking a patriotic society but rather a social welfare organization. Shortly after the war an obscure newspaper, *Dopolavoro,* was founded in Rome by Mario Giani to encourage working people to make profitable use of their free hours. The newspaper grew into a workingmen's society similar to the Y.M.C.A. and was gradually drawn

[11] A statement by Augusto Turati.

[12] *Regolamento Piccole Italiane e Giovani Italiane* (Rome: Libreria del Littorio, pp. 11–12).

[13] *Foglio d'Ordini,* April 20, 1928.

under the Fascist wing as a part of the party's general scheme to attract and aid the lower classes.[14]

Dopolavoro has become a semipublic institution with 278,308 members—39.25 per cent of the total labor population in Italy. Dopolavoro performs all those functions which are common to organizations of its kind. It fosters sports, arranges excursions, builds theaters, and organizes theatrical companies among workers, trains orchestras and choruses, holds both cultural and professional night schools, and furnishes motion pictures. Each of its numerous branches (there are Dopolavoro groups in almost all towns of any size) stresses that part of the program which is most attractive to its members. According to statistics assembled in 1927, 62.37 per cent of the members take part in sports, 34.75 per cent in various sorts of recreation, 27.12 per cent in the excursions, 25.30 per cent in the night schools, 16.38 in the dramatic groups, and 16.38 in the musical organizations.[15] These figures are not meaningless. Dopolavoro plays a large part in the lives of Italian workers. Its athletics have taken on national importance; its dramatic efforts (usually guided by professionals) result in good amateur productions, and its excursions have stimulated traveling among the lower classes of Italians. That the work of the organization may be more successful, state services (railways, steamships, etc.) and most large business houses give Dopolavoro members reductions varying from 10 to 50 per cent.

To be sure, Dopolavoro is not engaged directly in patriotic or Fascist propaganda, but an organization of its kind is bound to soften the hearts of those it serves if they happen to be hostile to the régime. Dopolavoro is clearly

[14] Laws of May 1, 1925, and March 18, 1926.

[15] *Opera Nazionale Dopolavoro, Bollettino Mensile,* December, 1927, p. 39.

attached to Fascism. Its former president, the Duke of
Aosta, has been replaced by the secretary of the party,
Augusto Turati, thus guaranteeing a Fascist "spirit"
among its central and local officials.

3. *The National Foundation for the Protection and
Aid of Mothers and Children.*—The Foundation for the
Protection and Aid of Mothers and Children was created
by the Fascists in order to centralize all social welfare
work of this sort. A percentage of the compulsory syndicate dues is applied toward its support. The Fascists
are interested in increasing the Italian population not
only by augmenting the birth-rate but also by caring for
infants and children. The society is simply a part of a
demographic movement for a "greater" Italy.

4. *Sports.*—Since the advent of Fascism sports in Italy have taken a new lease on life. In almost every field
of activity one sees evidence of this fact. We have commented upon the large place given to physical education
both in the youth organizations and in Dopolavoro. The
same holds true of the Fascist university groups and of
the more professedly athletic associations (such as the
Alpine clubs), and of the army. As a result of their experience during the war, Italian military authorities have
come to recognize the importance of sound physical training, with the result that sports play a large part in military training. A school has been created to prepare athletic instructors for the army and navy.

The organization which oversees all this athletic activity is the National Italian Olympic Committee. Fascism at first tried to foster sports by means of a new organization, the National Association for Physical Education, but had little success and now lends all its moral
and financial support to the endeavors of the Olympic

Committee. One third of the taxes on all sorts of public performances are turned over to this organization and every encouragement possible is given for the construction of new stadiums and gymnasiums. The magnificent stadium at Bologna, Il Littoriale, and the Fascist school for teachers of physical education at Rome are examples of the results of such a policy. Italian athletes receive the moral support of the government. When the Italian Olympic team left for the games in 1928, the secretary of the party addressed a stirring appeal to its members urging them to do their best—in the Fascist manner.

The new importance attached to sports has had its results. Italy has produced some of the world's best soccer teams in recent years; her tennis team was runner-up in the Davis Cup Tournament (European division) in 1928, and in general the Italian youth show signs of physical education. A healthy nation is a stronger nation, say the Fascists.

5. *Veterans' associations.*—Another patriotic and philanthropic society is the National Association of Veterans.[16] It was created in 1919 (but reorganized in 1923) for the purpose of keeping alive the cult of the nation, of nourishing the patriotic memories of the war, of glorifying the fallen heroes, and of giving financial aid to veterans restored to civil life. The association opened its doors to all those who had participated in the war and in 1927 had a membership of 469,671 in Italy and 8,916 abroad.[17] During the first years of Fascism this organization was not particularly friendly to the Régime, even going so far as openly to join the opposition at its Con-

[16] *L'Associazione Nazionale fra i Combattenti.* Headquarters: Palazzo Venezia, Rome.

[17] "Bilancio di un Anno di honoro della Associazione Nazionale Combattenti," in *Italia Augusta,* February, 1928, p. 90.

gress at Assisi in 1924.[18] In March of the next year, however, the Fascists took control of the association and imposed on it a Triumvirate Directory named by Mussolini. At its meeting in 1927 the National Council of the association voted a resolution from which the following is quoted:

Realizing that the National Association of Veterans, the stern custodian of the spirit of sacrifice and heroism of the Great War, has finally harmonized the spirits and intentions, the ardor and the passion of the Italians of the trenches, and has become an efficacious instrument of patriotic education and of material assistance and has thus become a living and working force which the Nation and the Régime can surely rely upon in every crisis;

[The Association] presents to Benito Mussolini, the Chief, Creator and *Duce* of Fascist Italy and of the new civilization which has resulted from the labors of the War and of the Revolution, the homage, fidelity, and devotion of the National Association of Veterans, ready at his call for all sacrifices and all acts of bravery. . . .

Aside from its patriotic and militarist nature the association carries on important social work in co-operation with the National Foundation for Veterans *(L'Opera Nazionale per i Combattenti)*, an organization which was founded in 1917, but which did little until the middle of 1919.[19] These institutions have provided small credits for veterans, have opened professional schools, have furnished legal advice, have carried on campaigns against tuberculosis and malaria, have co-operated with other organizations in realizing sanitary improvements, and have supported needy veterans.

Perhaps the most important work, however, has been of an agricultural nature, especially that of the National Foundation for Veterans. Its patrimony is valued at 350

[18] Giorgio Pini and Federico Bresadola, *Storia del Fascismo* (Rome: Libreria del Littorio, 1928), p. 410.

[19] Headquarters: Via Ulpiano Il, Rome. Organ: *Italia Augusta* (monthly).

million lire.[20]. It has taken over 50,000 hectares of land, 25,000 to be sold in small lots to veterans and 25,000 to be improved (drained or irrigated) by the foundation itself. Already over 80 million lire have been spent for this work.[21] In addition to this task an attempt has been made to improve agriculture by furnishing instruction to farmers through lectures and motion pictures, chiefly by means of the itinerary motion-picture trucks which reach the most secluded regions. Attempts have also been made to colonize certain parts of Italy; veterans especially have been encouraged to go to South Tyrol to spread the Italian language among the German-speaking population, and also to settle in certain depopulated districts of the South.[22] In these ways veterans are aided and influenced and at the same time used to contribute to the moral and economic strength of the nation.

Still another institution composed of war veterans is the National Association of War Cripples and Invalids,[23] which has been given the exclusive right to represent those who were wounded in the war.[24] Although it has remained above party politics and is in theory not Fascist[25] it is very patriotic. Its main purposes are (a) to "maintain among the wounded a pride in the sacrifice and a sentiment of fraternity in the love of the Nation; (b) to educate the people to a sense of duty adequate to the great destinies of the Nation; (c) to give its members both

[20] *Almanacco delle Forze Armate* (1927), p. 942.

[21] *Op. cit.,* pp. 948.50. These figures are for the year ending in 1926.

[22] Every issue of *Italia Augusta* carries a long list of advertisements of real estate in South Tyrol which may be purchased by veterans.

[23] *L'Associazione Nazionale fra i Mutilati ed Invalidi di Guerra;* president: Carlo Delcroix; founded in April, 1917.

[24] Royal Decree of April 19, 1923.

[25] Giorgio Pini and Federico Bresadola, *Storia del Fascismo,* p. 403.

moral and material aid by all means which inspire social solidarity. . . . ."[26] During the last months of the war the Association's Committees of Action greatly contributed toward keeping up the morale of the army at the front. Since the war it has carried on a ceaseless campaign of patriotic propaganda among its 300,000 members. Thanks to its efforts the question of pensions has been satisfactorily solved. The president, Delcroix, who was blinded in service, is one of the most popular and eloquent orators in Italy today.

[26] *Almanacco delle Forze Armate* (1927), p. 765.

CHAPTER XI
THE USE OF SYMBOLISM
AND TRADITION

1. *Political symbols.*—By no means the least cause of Fascism's rapid rise and uncanny power is its imaginative appeal. It is a genuine religion and has used all the techniques of a religious cult. We have already discussed this phase of Fascism in so far as it has direct bearing on Catholicism and the Roman church. It remains to indicate some of the more secular and political symbols by which Fascism has established its hold on the imagination of the people.

The original connotations of the word *fascio* were quite innocent. It had two meanings. In one sense it was simply a colorless term like group, band, club, or circle, denoting that these associations were primarily neither political nor military. The *fasci* were simply groups or nuclei of young men banded together for a particular purpose. Thus there were *fasci* of interventionists (prowar groups) in 1915, futurist *fasci,* revolutionary *fasci,* nationalist *fasci,* etc. Fascism, therefore, was in its origins and motivation a movement of non-political local groups banded together for non-political action. It was, as the phrase went, "antiparty" in spirit. Hence there was strong opposition within the ranks when the leaders decided in 1921 to transform the movement into a political party. Strictly speaking, "Fascist party" is a contradiction in terms.

In a more particular sense the word *fascio* signifies the bundle of rods inclosing an axe which was carried by the Roman lictors as a symbol of authority, discipline, and power. The rods had been administered for minor insubordination and the axe for capital crimes. The adoption of this Roman symbol of the lictor's rods, known as the *littorio,* was little more than an etymological *tour de force;* but the idea behind it took hold rapidly. The symbol, therefore, suggested an extra-legal principle of authority and the appeal to the force of disciplined action as the ultimate basis of political power and cohesion. The correlative idea is that of dux *(il duce),* the leader who carries the *littorio* and embodies its authority and strength. During the parliamentary strife of Fascism, the *littorio* naturally was adopted as the party symbol, though the Fascists protested continually that it could never be a *party* symbol in theory, since it stood for the authority of a whole united people. After the march on Rome, this idea was insisted on quite literally and the adjective "Fascist" was used as more inclusive in meaning than the adjective "nationalist." It was held to represent the idea of a morally united people, conscious of a single national will. Hence state organs and official bodies were all called Fascist and in 1927 the *littorio* was legally made the emblem of state, along with the flag. It must appear on all official documents and is, of course, displayed on all political occasions. It has obtained a great vogue in artistic designs, having been worked into innumerable Fascist publication covers, for example, and the architecture of the victory monument at Bolzano, and public buildings, such as the Labor Office and Libreria del Littorio at Rome.

The party badge or pin can be worn only by the million or so members of the Fascist party. It is a gold pin representing the *littorio* against a tri-color background. Members of the Fascist confederations wear a similar pin, but the *littorio* is replaced by a map of Italy. The use of the *littorio* for unofficial purposes is now forbidden by law. Since the doors of the party have been closed, it is regarded as a badge of honor and privilege to be able to display the party pin. Politicians and office-seekers are especially given to displaying it on all occasions.

Along with the *littorio* goes the black flag of the *fasci*. This pennant was taken over from the *arditi* or post-war legionnaires led by d'Annunzio. Theoretically it must be honored as a national flag, but practically it receives less respect than the tri-color. When Fascists parade, however, they expect the usual salutes and doffing of hats when the black standards and pennants pass by.

2. *Fascist uniforms and rituals.*—The uniform of the Fascist militia is also adapted from that of the *arditi*. Mazzini, I believe, began the fashion of wearing black as a sign of national mourning. With the *arditi* the black shirt became the symbol of national enthusiasm and military daring. Originally the black shirt and tie was accompanied by the black fez and this is still the formal headdress—either the true Turkish fez or a modification of it. But the most common headgear is the service hat, similar to that worn by the Alpine corps in the war. It is of the olive-tan color of the army and militia uniforms. The hats have triangular chevrons or stripes sewed on them to indicate rank. The Fascist militia uniform is strikingly "snappy" and severe. Black leather belts and puttees are worn, accompanied by the ever conspicuous automatic revolver. Most Fascists take considerable pride in their appearance. Of course, the uniform is used only for active service, during mobilization or on parade. The black shirt, however, is very popular even with civilian dress.

The uniforms of the Fascist juvenile organizations

are similar to those of the Fascist militiamen. The girls wear black skirts, white "middies" with black emblems on them, white gloves, black caps. They may be seen frequently marching to school in uniform, swinging their books in a military manner, and presenting a very athletic appearance. Hikes and marches similar to those of the Boy and Girl Scouts in America are very popular.

The Fascist salute is supposedly a revival of the Roman salute. The whole arm is raised forward and upward at an angle of about forty-five degrees, the palm of the hand out straight and stiff. Sometimes the salute is performed with grace and dignity, but usually it is either excessively vigorous and awkward or slovenly and formless. The former attitude is common among the boys, the latter is conspicuous among politicians and officials. Doormen, porters, etc., in public employ have taken up with the custom and are apt to carry it to ridiculous lengths. The salute is most effective when made by soldiers in mass formation or by a large crowd at a public gathering.

The yell, *"eia, eia, a-la-lá!"* which may accompany the salute is used vigorously, much as college boys use their yells. The Fascist anthem, "Giovinezza," is a rollicking, carefree student song which became popular during the war. It is a good marching tune but hardly suitable for the heroic words which have been given to it. The original student song runs:

> Son finiti i giorni lieti
> Degli studi e degli amori:
> O campagni in alto i cuori,
> E il passato salutiam!
>
> È la vita una battaglia,
> E il cammino irto d'inganni,
> Ma siam forti, abbiam vent 'anni,
> L'avvenire non temiam.

Giovinezza, giovinezza
Primavera di bellezza,
Della vita nell 'asprezza
Il tuo canto squilla e va!

This is true to the general spirit of the tune. The Fascist
version runs:

Salve, o popolo d'Eroi,
Salve, o Patri immortale!
Son rinati i figli tuoi
Con la fe' nell 'ideale.

Il valor de' tuoi guerrieri,
La virtù dei pionieri,
La vision de l'Alighieri
Oggi brilla in tutti i cuor.

Giovinezza, giovinezza
Primavera di bellezza,
Nel fascimo è la salvezza
Della nostra libertá.

There have been several attempts to formulate official decalogues, creeds, etc., but these have been generally
regarded as too sacrilegious to be adopted. There are,
however, numerous "spiritual" manuals and handbooks
for Fascists and even more for the Advance Guard.[1]

3. *Holidays and celebrations.*—The Fascists have im-
itated the French revolutionary leaders in instituting a
Fascist calendar. Year I began in October, 1922. Suc-
cessive years are given a Roman numeral usually written
after the Christian date. All official documents must bear
the numeral of the Fascist year.

The general holidays and celebrations which have
been added to the calendar by the Fascists are the following:

[1] A specimen of this kind of literature was given in chap. iv, pp. 75–76.

(1) October 28, anniversary of the march on Rome:
This is usually celebrated by Fascist "marches" or parades, by a huge gathering in the Colosseum at Rome followed by a march to the Piazza Colonna where Mussolini addresses the crowd. Mussolini's speech is the only one allowed on that day throughout Italy. The day is primarily for the celebration of the militia. It is followed by several general military holidays.

(2) The nearest Sunday to March 23 is the *Leva Fascista*. On this day the graduates of the Advance Guard are initiated into the *fasci*. The symbols of the initiation, party membership cards, and rifles (to signify membership in the militia) are presented to the young men. The day is in general devoted to a celebration for the juvenile organizations. The chief ceremony takes place at Rome in the Piazza del Popolo, where the national heads of the party officiate.

(3) April 21, the birthday of Rome. This is Fascist Labor Day, taking the place of the forbidden May first celebration. The syndicates have their parades, speeches, and general festivities on this day.

In addition to these new Fascist celebrations, there are the traditional patriotic holidays. The *Statuto* is celebrated by devoting the first Sunday of June to a glorification of Italian unification by elaborate military parades. On November 4—the anniversary of the World War victory, November 11—Armistice Day, and on the king's birthday similar military celebrations take place. The queen's birthday, the anniversary of the taking of Rome (September 20), and the anniversary of the declaration of war (May 24) are minor events on the patriotic calendar. There is a tendency toward allowing the specifically Fascist celebrations to eclipse the enthusiasm and display on these older holidays, but how far this will go is as yet difficult to tell. At present it is obvious that the government encourages anything which keeps the patriotic emotions aroused.

Then there are special celebrations from time to time. In 1928, for example, in connection with the celebration of October 28, a large sum of war debt certificates was burned on an ancient Roman altar, taken from the museum for that purpose and placed on the steps of the Victor Emmanuel monument near the tomb of the Unknown Soldier.

There are occasional celebrations in connection with the various economic "battles" which the government is waging. Prizes, for example, are distributed with great display for the best grain produced in the agricultural campaign known as "the battle of the wheat."

4. *Romanism.*—The tradition which is most exploited by Fascism is that of the ancient Roman Empire. Examples of Roman symbolism have already been mentioned. But Rome is to be revived not merely in externals, but in the intellectual temper and moral fiber of Fascist "culture" and empire. Much of this Romanism has been taken over from the d'Annunzian nationalists, but the Fascists have carried the theme further than d'Annunzio ever dreamed. The militia is organized like the ancient Roman army: legions, cohorts, centuries, and maniples. The old standards and titles are being revived. The severe "marches" and martial discipline of the youth are supposed to rekindle the moral vigor and stamina of the traditional Roman. The ideals and the burden of empire are being revived. Even Roman religion, in so far as it is not offensive to Roman Catholicism, is preached as an intrinsic aspect of Italian spiritual genius. Latin is being revived in the school curriculum, Latin dramas are given in old Roman amphitheaters, and Roman art is be-

ing encouraged. An effort is being made to give the city of Rome an appearance of "the eternal city," to make it cosmopolitan, imperial, and impressive. There is much talk of Caesarism and though Mussolini has not assumed the title, he is regarded as literally carrying on the work of the Caesars, and is frequently pictured in the pose and garb of one of them.

5. *Other traditions used by Fascism.*—It is impossible to enter here into a detailed account of the various other intellectual and political traditions which Fascism has exploited. Naturally anything which is glorious in Italy's past is regarded as a fitting predecessor and prefiguration of Fascism. To mention only the most significant:

(1) The *risorgimento* is now pictured by Fascist historians as beginning the spiritual and political rebirth of Italy which Fascism is completing: Especially the Republican and Liberal elements in Fascism exalt Mazzini as the great pre-Fascist. There are, of course, Fascists who think the opposite,[2] who regard Fascism as anti-*risorgimento,* as a return to the ancient and indigenous Italian traditions which the all-too-French *risorgimento* tried to undo. But on the whole the Fascists are content to stand on the shoulders of Mazzini and Garibaldi.

(2) The policy of imperialism or Africanism, represented by Francesco Crispi, is used by the Fascists as a traditional basis for their foreign policy and a traditional sanction for their expansiveness: This political tradition is accompanied by an elaborate philosophy of history and an inflated conception of Italy's rightful and inevitable place in the sun.

(3) Fascism has not hesitated to place emphasis on the great cultural contributions which Italy has made to

[2] Cf. Curzio Malaparte.

the world: It was Rome which gave the French and the Spanish their languages, which put its impress on Christianity, which contributed the many Italian saints and the Roman hierarchy, and it was Italian "spiritual imperialism" which carried the church throughout Western Europe. It was Dante who produced the greatest poetry of the medieval period. It was the Italian renaissance, with its Giotto, Michelangelo, Leonardo da Vinci, and Raphael, that broke the spell of the "Dark Ages." And now after a brief respite Italy is again to become the great center of light. Thus do Fascists preach the cultural pre-eminence of their country. Nor has their faith been limited to words. There is a new zeal for spreading Italian culture abroad—witness the increasing number of Italian books exported and advertised and the creation of such Italian cultural centers as the Casa Italiana in New York City.

(4) Fascism represents itself as the embodiment of the World War in Italy: A typical Fascist is supposed to be an ardent war veteran (preferably wounded), a real soldier in training and in spirit. This is, of course, not a true picture; many Fascists took no part in the war and many veterans are not Fascists. But Fascists regard it as one of their prime duties and functions to uphold the honor and glory of Italy's rôle in the war. They seek to personify the war spirit of Italy and to defend her war aims. They take credit for pushing Italy into the war and think of their post-war activities as simply a fulfilment of the policy and aims of the war.

(5) There are several elements of the syndicalist and socialist traditions which Fascism has embodied into its ideology: The Fascist emphasis on the *popolo d'Italia* is in part a survival of the idea of national solidarity handed down by the *risorgimento,* and in part an appeal

to the Italian proletariat. The people is to be vindicated on the one hand against the parasitical internal bourgeoisie which had its stronghold in the Liberal government, and on the other against plutocratic foreign powers. Italy is pictured as a proletarian nation waging a class struggle against an international plutocracy. The syndicalistic prejudices against "political action" are exploited in this connection, and Italy is told that she must use economic weapons and ultimately military violence. The socialistic idea of the solidarity of the proletariat is thus used to bolster nationalism, and the severer the hardships the more urgent the need of patriotism and loyalty.

(6) In this connection there is some exploitation of the Napoleonic tradition: just as Napoleon is supposed to have embodied and spread the ideals of the French Revolution, so Mussolini is regarded as the vindicator of the Italian people in the eyes of the world. Mussolini's attempts to assume a Napoleonic personal appearance are familiar to everyone. On the whole, however, this Napoleonic pose is for foreign consumption; within Italy Fascism aims to resemble a revival of ancient Rome, not an imitation of nineteenth-century France. The theory is that Fascism marks the end of the epoch of the French Revolution and the beginning of a Roman epoch.

CHAPTER XII

GENERAL SURVEY

From the various facts considered in the foregoing chapters it may be possible now to draw the chief outlines of the pictures presented by Fascist citizenship. The feature above all others which singles out Fascism as a unique experiment is that it asserts an ancient ideal to be realized by modern methods: the ends are Roman and the means are up to date; the sovereign state dreamed by Dante and Machiavelli is to be achieved by economic and political devices invented since the French Revolution. Such a marriage of the old and new, such an attempt to make opposites meet, presents the fundamental conflicts and confusions of modern civilization in their most paradoxical and challenging aspect. Fascism, as they say, is a revolutionary conservatism or a conservative revolution.

The ancient ends may be summarized under the headings of national independence and unity, imperial power, centralized government, and Roman-Catholic civilization. This last term is, of course, difficult to define because the thing it denotes is itself highly complex and confused. It is not identical with the Catholic church, for it includes a traditional and widespread anticlericalism (in the name of Catholicism) ; it is neither Roman nor feudal, neither pagan nor Christian; it is a loose mixture of all these elements. All that can be said about it is that it is not a modern creation; its ideals and its institutions are the product of centuries of turbulent experience and several distinct civilizations. To a foreigner it seems an-

199

tique, to an Italian it is second nature. The present attempt to preserve this ancient order by means of the very forces which during the last century have threatened its undoing is a daring and instructive experiment in statecraft.

The modern means, just mentioned, may be summarized under the general institutions of militarism, capitalism, syndicalism, machinery, the press, and the public school. The aim of our investigation has been to see what changes have been instituted by Fascism in the functioning of these modern mechanisms, when they are made to serve purposes for which they were not invented.

To begin with the press and the school: in democratic countries, or at least in terms of the democratic ideas of the English and French revolutions, these institutions are supposed to be agencies for the formation and expression of public opinion on public issues. They are geared to the education of the individual citizen (the "reader"), who is supposed to find in them the requisite organs for informing himself about public affairs and expressing his approval or disapproval of the way in which they are being conducted by his government. Under the Fascist Régime, on the contrary, these institutions are consciously given a different function. The school is essentially the place where a newcomer becomes initiated into the traditions of his people, and the press is the agency whereby the government informs the people of "the national will" and appeals to it for support. In theory, the Fascist school and press are created (or tolerated) by the state to keep the people loyal to the state. They are essentially organs of propaganda, not of criticism. It follows that public opinion is essentially a matter of emotion rather than of information. Political *issues* are technical and their discussion is reserved for the politically competent.

Political aims are public and the whole people is urged to share in their expression. The people celebrate their ideals; the government does its best to choose the proper means for their realization. Moral enthusiasm on the one hand and technical competence on the other—this is an ancient and familiar philosophy. But it is interesting to see this philosophy of benevolent despotism, this division of labor based on the separation of means and end, applied thoroughly to modern institutions. We have attempted to show in the preceding chapters some of the details of this process. This involves a radical revision of the very idea of citizenship. Fascist citizenship is expressed, theoretically, not by the democratic machinery of public debate and suffrage on concrete issues but by an intelligent and industrious pursuit of one's own business. The government, theoretically, decides whether or not a given profession or business is valuable to the state and nation. If it is, it is legally recognized and protected by the national syndicates and corporations to which it belongs. It thus becomes more than a private enterprise, it is genuinely public service, and it is a political duty to perform this particular service or function well. In other words, just as the integration of the state is essentially economic (the corporative state) so the exercise of citizenship is also economic. The state demands that I mind my own business! Conversely, my *operosità,* my diligence, is the test of my devotion to my country.

There is another fundamental aspect of this economic conception of citizenship. Since the nation is, theoretically, an economic unit, any economic success or failure is shared by all its members. Hence the experience of hard times, high cost of living, or other hardship is a patriotic sacrifice demanded by the exigencies of international competition and is not to be regarded as a pretext for censuring the government. Rather, the harder the times, the more loyalty is demanded. This transformation of class struggle into international struggle makes a political asset, for Fascism, out of the very factor of economic discontent which democratic governments most dread. The economic life is militarized and business is literally a form of warfare. How far such ideas can succeed in practice, remains to be seen, but, the *idea* is at least clear and is already being put to the practical test.

The net effect of all this is to integrate economic groups for national business and to erect barriers for international economic grouping. The kind of international relations favored by this idea is identical with that engaged in between private corporations, namely, the negotiations of specific trade agreements, bargains, contracts, and other usual forms of business competition.

The problem of traditional regional groups and local loyalties is much simpler. It is not difficult to encourage region to vie with region, city with city, in national patriotism! Florence will try to outdo Perugia in demonstrations of loyalty to Mussolini, and Tuscany will vie with Umbria in courting the favor of the central government. Thus regional differences can be used to cement national unity—just as in the United States municipal teams serve to glorify baseball. Here all depends on the maintenance of morale in the local *fascio*. Just as any military organization centers attention on the fighting spirit of each company, so Fascism makes discipline within the ranks of the *fascio* the crucial measure of its strength as a national régime. Any evidence of local disturbances is immediately followed by a "shake-up" and each official is held strictly responsible for the morale of his district. But so long as the morale is maintained and so long as all eyes are centered on Rome, all sorts of regional differences are not only tolerated but explicitly encouraged. For example, although it is general Fascist policy to advertise nationalistic poets like d'Annunzio and national saints like St. Francis, the government does not hesitate to patronize anyone who makes himself locally famous (e.g., the local-color novelists, local military heroes, or the patron saints of communities), on the ground that any distinction achieved by any Italian anywhere is a tribute to the genius of the Italian people. Fascist politicians are more alert than modernist artists in realizing that Italians will continue to prefer in politics, as in art, richness of internal diversity to the austere simplicity of the Romans.

The fundamental conflict, however, between state and church, for the devotion and resources of the Italian people, is a more serious problem. As has been pointed out in the foregoing, this problem transcends the relatively simple issue of the political relations between church and state, an issue which has probably been solved for some years to come by the recent concordat and treaty; and it involves the more general dualism in modern life, especially in Italian life, between religion and politics, between the orthodox Christian version of the spiritual life and the growing secular interests of modern society. Most Italians claim allegiance to both of these realms, scarcely realizing any contradiction or conflict between them. But among the intellectual classes the conflict is acute. It is impossible to conceal the fact that both church and state want to be sovereign in the affections and minds of Italians, that both are appealing for the financial and moral support of their respective interests and that each feels the competition of the other. Certainly the Fascist Régime has made an enormous advance over its immediate predecessors in appealing to the religious imagination of

the people and in providing the nation with concrete symbols and forms for the expression of its political faith.
For the younger generation and for the militant spirits
in Italy Fascism provides a vigorous and stimulating
mode of life, and its appeal will probably continue as long
as Italians remain conscious of the necessity of competing with foreign powers and interests. Fascism rests fundamentally on the basis of international struggle. If, for
any reason, Italians should seek more intimate relations
with international groups, if their loyalty should become
less exclusively national, or if internal class struggles
should become too acute, Fascist methods and ideals of
civic training will have little relevance and small chance
of adapting themselves to such aims. In the meantime,
however, an emergency of a quite different nature has
been met, and the methods employed may serve to in-
struct those peoples who have as yet evaded such emergencies.

BIBLIOGRAPHICAL NOTE

The most important works concerning Fascist civic training have been mentioned in footnotes. A complete bibliography concerning Fascism is: G. Santangelo and C. Bracale, *Guida Bibliografica del Fascismo* (Rome: Libreria del Littorio, 1928). This may be supplemented by the monthly *Bibliografia Fascista,* published by the Libreria del Littorio, Rome.

Good bibliographies of the more important works concerning Fascism may be found in *Civiltà Fascista* (Turin: U.T.E.T., 1928), and Herbert W. Schneider, *Making the Fascist State* (New York: Oxford University Press, 1928).

Bibliographical service concerning Fascism is furnished by the Libreria del Littorio, Rome; Instituto Bibliografico Italiano, Florence; and the Centre International d'Etudes sur le Fascisme, Lausanne, Switzerland.

INDEX

INDEX

Academy, Italian, 109
Agenzia Stefani, 165
Agriculture, 9 ff.
Albania, 55
Alpini, 119
Army, 113
Army, associations of the, 124
Associazione Nazionale per gli Interessi del Mezzogiorno, 34
Austria, 45
Avanguardia, 112, 122, 179 ff.
Avanti, 166
Aviation, 127 f.
Azione Cattolica, 78

Balbo, Italo, 122
Balilla, 78, 112, 179 ff.
Bersaglieri, 119
Blue Ribbon, Institution of, 125
Bolzano, 36, 37, 44
Bottai, Giuseppe, 136, 169
Boy Scouts, Catholic, 78
Bureaucracy, 129 ff.

Cantalupo, 49, 61
Carabinieri, 119
Catholic church, 63 ff., 70 ff.
Church and state, 68, 203
Civil mobilization, 116
Collective contracts, 4, 21–22
Colonies, 56
Committee for the Diffusion of Italian Culture Abroad, 61 ff.
Confederazione Generale del Lavoro, 28
Confederation of Industry, 4
Confederations, National Fascist, 5
Co-operatives, 8
Coppola, 49
Conquista dello Stato, La, 168
Corporate Parliament, 6 f., 156
Corporate state, 4 ff.
Corporations, Ministry of, 6, 136
Corradini, Enrico, 49

Corriere della Sera, 165
Credaro, 36, 38
Critica Fascista, 169
Croats, 46
Croce, Benedetto, 63, 109
Crown of Italy, Order of, 125

D'Annunzio, 28, 46 f., 49
Dante Alighieri, 60
De Stefani, 14 f.
Diaz, General, 121
Diritto del Lavoro, Il, 170
Dopolavoro, 182 ff.
Duce, 190

Economic groups, 3
Economics, Fascist policy, 14 ff., 142, 201 f.
Education, 37, 41, 83 ff.
Electoral Reform of 1924, 140
Electoral Reform of 1928, 156

Fanciulli Cattolici, 78
Farinacci, 145, 167
Fasci, 28, 140, 150 ff., 189
Fasci, Foreign, 57 ff.
Fascism, 30, 48, 73, 142 f., 199, 204
Fascist Faculty of Political Science of Perugia, 108
Fascist party, 26 f., 40, 140 ff., 191
Fascist party and regionalism, 26 f., 32 ff.
Fascist party, Constitution of, 146 f.
Fascist party, Grand Council of, 147 f., 157
Fascist party, membership of, 155
Fascist University of Bologna, 109, 170
Federzoni, 37, 49, 145, 169
Fiume, 46 f.
Foglio d'Ordini, 152 f., 167 f.
Foreign policy, 48 ff.
Forges-Davanzati, 49, 167
France, 53 ff.
Free Masonry, 66 f.

Gentile, 145
Gentile School Reform, 41, 65, 84 ff., 109
Gerarchia, 169
Germans, 34, 46
Giolitti, 158
Giornale d'Italia, 165
Giovani Italiane, 182
Giovinezza, 193
Grandi, Dino, 49

Holidays, 153 f., 194 ff.

Imperialism, 54, 57, 61 ff., 126
Impero, L', 167
Internationalism and Fascism, 50 ff.

Jugo-Slavia, 55

Labor Charter, 4 ff., 132
Labor tribunals, 6
Ladinos, 34 f.
Lavoro d'Italia, Il, 167
League of Nations, 50 ff.
Leva Fascista, 122
Libreria del Littorio, 171 f.
Literacy statistics, 83 f.
Little Entente, 55 ff.
Littorio, 190 f.
Lockouts, 6
London, Pact of, 46
Luce, 173 f.

Mafia, 53 f.
Maraviglia, 49
Marinetti, 29, 63, 167
Mercantilism, neo-, 15 ff.
Militarism, 110 ff.
Militarism and patriotism, 114
Military expenditures, 111
Military training, 111 ff.
Mondo, Il, 166
Motion pictures, 173 ff.
Mussolini, Arnaldo, 164, 166
Mussolini, Benito, 29, 37, 45, 61, 63, 110, 112, 122, 125, 137, 143, 146, 159, 166, 176, 198

National Fascist Association of Primary School Teachers, 103
National Fascist Institute of Culture, 109, 170

National Fascist Syndicate of Journalists, 159, 163 f.
National Foundation for the Protection and Aid of Mothers and Children, 184
Nationalists, 49
Naval League, 125
Navy, 125 ff.
Nettuno, Treaty of, 55
News, Control of, 160

Officers, Army, 117 ff.
Osservatore Romano, 165 f.

Parliamentary Reform, 156
Pasella, 3
Penal Code, 66
Piccole Italiane, 182
Politica, La, 49, 169
Popolo d'Italia, Il, 166
Popularist party, 28
Prefects, Circular to the, 137
Press, control of, 160 ff.
Press, the, 42, 159 ff., 200
Preszzolini, Giuseppe, 97
Price-fixing, 6
Provincial Economic Councils, 6
Public Employees, General Fascist Association of, 131 f., 134 ff.

Regionalism, 24 ff., 202
Religion, 63 ff.
Rocco, 4, 37, 49, 133, 169
Rossoni, 4

San Rapallo, Treaty of, 46
Santissima Annunziata, Supreme Order of, 124
Sarfatti, Magherita, 169
Savoy, Military Order of, 125
School System, Administration of, 87 f.
Schools, elementary, 89, 91, 201
Schools, secondary, 89
Slovenes, 46
Social insurance, 9
South Tyrol, 34 ff.
Sports, 184 f.
Squadrism, 31, 144
SS. Maurizio and Lazzaro, Order of, 124
Stampa, La, 165
Stirpe, La, 170

Strikes, 6
Sturzo, Don, 77 f.
Suckert, Curzio, 168
Syndicalism, 4 ff., 19 ff.
Syndicates, 3
Symbolism, 189 ff.

Teachers, 102, 105
Textbook Commission, 93 f.
Textbooks, 94 ff., 98 ff., 104 f.
Tolomei, Dr. Ettore, 36, 38, 41
Traditions, 195 ff.
Tribuna, La, 167

Trieste, 46 ff.
Tunis, 54
Turati, Augusto 118, 145

Uniforms, Fascist, 191 f.
Universities, 106

Vatican, Pact of, 70 ff.
Venetia-Julia, 46
Versailles, Peace of, 50
Voce, La, 172
Volpi, 15

War Veterans Associations, 44, 185 ff.

[PRINTED
IN U·S·A·]

3782